T0096635

CZECH OPEN 2016

27th INTERNATIONAL CHESS AND GAMES FESTIVAL

Pardubice 14th – 31st July 2016, the Czech Republic

www.czechopen.net

- **Rating tournaments with rating for FIDE** (open grand master tournament, 4 open FIDE tournaments, Open Championship of the Czech Republic of 4-member team tournament)
- **Rapid tournaments** (open championship of the Czech Republic, tournaments for individuals, pairs and youngsters)
- **Blitz tournaments** (marathon, tournament with k.o. system, super blitz tournament 2 × 3 min, open tournaments for individuals, pairs and teams)
- **Untraditional chess disciplines** (problem solving competition, Fischerandom chess, Bughouse, Raindropchess, Polgar Superstar Chess, Basque chess)
- **Tournaments in other games** (bridge, go, draughts, backgammon, renju, gomoku, mancala games, ZATRE, shogi, Xiangqi usw.)
- **Rich accompanying programme** (small football tournament, bowling, table tennis, Sudoku competitions etc.)

**Total price fund of the festival
more than 25 000 EUR**

**Accommodation from 10 EUR,
meals in restaurants from 3,5 EUR**

EUROPEAN YOUTH CHAMPIONSHIP 2016

Categories boys and girls up to 8, 10, 12, 14, 16, and 18 years of age

Prague 17th – 28th August 2016, the Czech Republic

www.eycc2016.eu

CZECH TOUR 2016

16th International Chess Festivals Series

www.czechtour.net

CHESS SUMMER IN THE HEART OF EUROPE

14.–31. 7. 2016 27th CZECH OPEN (Pardubice)
Chess and Games Festival

5.–12. 8. 2016 3rd SUMMER PRAGUE OPEN
Open IM tournament and rating tournament with rating for FIDE

13.–20. 8. 2016 19th OLOMOUC CHESS SUMMER
Round robin GM and IM tournaments, seniors tournament over 60 years of age, rating tournament with rating for FIDE

CHESS SUMMER ON SUNNY BEACH

5.–13. 9. 2016 15th SUNNY BEACH OPEN (BULGARIA)
Open GM tournament, seniors tournament over 60 years of age, women tournament, tournament for children up to 12 years of age and 2 rating tournaments with rating for FIDE

WORLD SENIOR CHESS CHAMPIONSHIP 2016

Categories men and women 50+ and 65+

**Marianske Lazne (Marienbad)
18th November – 1st December 2016,
the Czech Republic**

Players can participate regardless of their rating.

www.wscc2016.net

„I have seen the whole India, Ceylon and all the spas of Europe, but I have been nowhere so smitten with the poetry of beautiful nature like here in Marianske Lazne," Edward VII, King of England (1841–1910).

AVE-KONTAKT s.r.o., Strossova 236, 530 03 Pardubice, Czech Republic
Tel. + 420 – 466 535 200, mobile phone + 420 - 608 203 007, e-mail: j.mazuch@avekont.cz

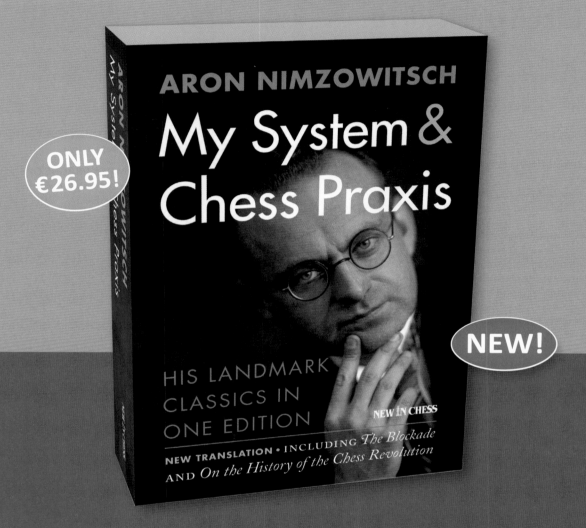

Komodo Chess 10

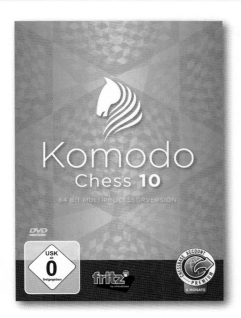

Komodo Chess 10*

The new number one has arrived! Thanks to a host of extensive improvements and fine tweaking, the latest version of Komodo has again gained over 60 Elo points on its predecessor. The changes cover several areas: the evaluation function has been significantly sharpened, particularly with respect to king safety and endgame positions, and the search algorithm has been improved and optimized to run on multiple processors. Komodo 10 is also better at managing its time, and just generally calculates faster.

The result is an unbeatable combination - the strongest chess engine ever running on the best and most popular user interface around. As it comes with the Fritz 15 GUI,

Komodo, as well as chess prowess, offers all the training and playing functions you know from Fritz, including direct access to the ChessBase Web Apps such as Live Database, the ChessBase video portal, our tactics server and more!

Komodo's intelligent and results-driven evaluations have also proven extremely effective in practice and are reflected in the engine's playing style. If Komodo 10 considers its position to be advantageous, it avoids exchanges and seeks to open the position, but when defending a worse position, it strives to exchange pieces and block the position, in an attempt to push the game towards a draw.

It also recently demonstrated its exceptional playing strength in a series of matches against grandmasters, including the current world #6, Hikaru Nakamura. Komodo remained unbeaten in over 50 games in which it gave its human opponents a material advantage or several free moves (with the exception of only a few games in which the handicap consisted of two important pawns or the f7 pawn and three free moves) - Komodo even beat Nakamura 2.5 to 1.5!

This ultra-strong engine has won three of the last four TCEC championships, making it a multiple winner of the most prestigious prize

in computer chess. What is more, at tournament time controls, Komodo is #1 in the majority of rating lists.

Komodo Chess 10 comes with:

- New 64-bit multi-processor engine

- Latest Fritz 15 64-bit user interface (optionally 32-bit)

- Premium membership for the all new ChessBase Web Apps and playchess.com (six months)

  Komodo Chess 10   79,90 €

System requirements:
Minimum: Pentium III 1 GHz, 2 GB AM, Windows XP (Service Pack 3), 7/8, DirectX9, graphics card with 256 MB RAM, DVD-ROM drive, Windows Media Player 9 and internet access for program activation. Playchess.com access, Let's Check and updates.

Recommended: PC Intel i5 (Quadcore), 4 GB RAM, Windows 8.1/10, DirectX10, graphics card with 512 MB RAM or more, 100% DirectX10- compatible sound card, Windows Media Player 11, DVD ROM drive and internet access for program activation, Let's Check, ChessBase Live Database, Engine Cloud, Tactics Training and updates.

* Available end of May 2016

CHESSBASE GMBH · OSTERBEKSTR. 90a · D-22083 HAMBURG · TEL ++(49) 40/639060-10 · WWW.CHESSBASE.COM · INFO@CHESSBASE.COM
CHESSBASE DEALER: INTERCHESS B.V., P. O. Box 1093, NL-1810 KB ALKMAAR, phone (++31)72 51 27 137, fax (++31)72 51 58 234, www.newinchess.com

"A terrific value for anyone interested in refurbishing and fine-tuning their opening repertoire."

-Chess Today

With lots of instructional exercises

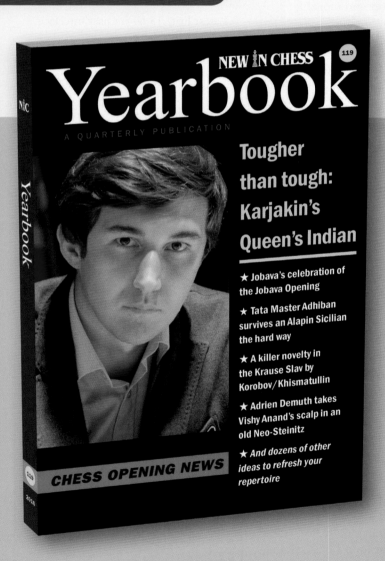

NEW IN CHESS 119

Yearbook

A QUARTERLY PUBLICATION

Tougher than tough: Karjakin's Queen's Indian

★ Jobava's celebration of the Jobava Opening

★ Tata Master Adhiban survives an Alapin Sicilian the hard way

★ A killer novelty in the Krause Slav by Korobov/Khismatullin

★ Adrien Demuth takes Vishy Anand's scalp in an old Neo-Steinitz

★ And dozens of other ideas to refresh your repertoire

CHESS OPENING NEWS

With answers to urgent questions such as:

- Why is everybody playing 1.c2-c4 these days?
- Which radical change did Wojtaszek initiate in the Rubinstein Nimzo-Indian?
- How to crush a 2700+ player in the Berlin?
- Why would you play the 'patzer check' 7.♕a4+ in the Exchange Grünfeld?
- With which risky sideline did Li Chao shake up a 2600+ player's Queen's Gambit?
- Which beautiful novelty did Denis Khismatullin introduce in the Krause Slav?
- How did Adrien Demuth beat Anand with black in a half-forgotten Neo-Steinitz?
- What tricky Alapin Sicilian should you avoid at all cost according to Adhiban Baskaran?
- What to do against 6.g3 in the Paulsen Variation?
- What is the big fun of Baadur Jobava's opening 1.d4, 2.♗f4, 3.♘c3 ?
- How did Vladimir Potkin surprise Wei Yi in the Hartston Variation of the Anti-Grünfeld?
- Is Black in trouble in Levon Aronian's pet line with 4...♗b4 in the English Four Knights?
- How does Wesley So deal with the Breyer Variation?
- What is Christian Bauer's way to get active with black against 1.b3?
- What is the sense of Magnus Carlsen's 9.♗b5 sortie in the Steinitz French?
- What can we learn from the World Champions in the Chigorin Spanish?
- And much more

Paperback ◆ 256 pages ◆ € 29.95 ◆ available at your local (chess)bookseller or at newinchess.com

'I've found out that when you feel well, you tend to play well.'

CONTRIBUTORS TO THIS ISSUE

Varuzhan Akobian, Levon Aronian, Jeroen Bosch, Fabiano Caruana, Anish Giri, Nils Grandelius, Pentala Harikrishna, John Henderson, Garry Kasparov, Mihail Marin, Dylan McClain, Parimarjan Negi, Peter Heine Nielsen, Maxim Notkin, Arthur van de Oudeweetering, Nazi Paikidze, Judit Polgar, Hans Ree, Matthew Sadler, Nigel Short, Maxime Vachier-Lagrave, Wesley So, Jan Timman

PHOTOS AND ILLUSTRATIONS

Lennart Ootes, Joachim Steinbru, Berend Vonk

COVER

Garry Kasparov: Lennart Ootes

'I also took some consolation in winning my mini-match against the incredibly speedy Nakamura, albeit thanks in part to his courteously allowing our game to continue when I had a "senior moment" touch move in our second-round game.' – *Garry Kasparov*

Bat, Ball & Chess

Baseball and chess were the first two pastimes to form national organizations in America. In 1857, the American Chess Association was formed, in 1858 the National Association of Baseball.

And in those formative years, famous chess players also took to baseball. In 1873, Captain George Henry Mackenzie captained a baseball team of New York chess players. In his youth, five-time US Champion Jackson Whipps Showalter was an acclaimed amateur pitcher in Kentucky, and famous for his curve ball (though contrary to belief, he did not invent it). In 1909, José Raul Capablanca attended Columbia University to play baseball, not chess. He played shortstop on the freshman team and considered turning professional — but a shoulder injury forced the switch to chess as a career.

And with chess becoming ingrained into the St. Louis community, an unusual sight in a 21st century Major League clubhouse has been the arrival for the St. Louis Cardinals of a chess table. It was a gift from Rex Sinquefield's Chess Club and Scholastic Center of Saint Louis to the chess-mad Cards manager Mike Matheny. And he says his players are bonding over chess, and now organizing tournaments before MLB games at Busch Stadium.

Because it's there

In 1923, when doomed English mountaineer George Mallory was asked by the *New York Times* why he wanted to climb Mount Everest, he famously replied: 'Because it's there'. Mallory's body lay frozen and undiscovered in a crevasse for more than 60 years after his attempt, and while there was another tragedy recently on Everest, we also got to

Jost Kobusch on his way to the chess club.

hear of a Himalayan Expedition that ended in good news and a checkmate.

Before 23-year-old German extreme mountaineer Jost Kobusch reached the 8,091 meter-high summit of Annapurna – one of the most dangerous mountains in the world via the north route – on 1 May, to become the youngest to do so, he played a game of chess against Israeli climber Nadav Ben-Yehuda just below the highest point. 'The idea came to us whilst we were in base camp', explained Jost in the latest *Adventure Sport* magazine. 'During the long periods of bad weather we spent our time playing chess and we said, if we make it to the summit, we will play a game of chess there.'

Nadav, who used bottled oxygen, reached the highest point just before Jost, who climbed without the aid of oxygen nor the help of any Sherpas. The two played blitz on a smartphone, 20 meters below the summit. But playing chess in extremely thin air at 8,000 meters without oxygen, says Jost, was 'as if you try drunken to solve a math problem: in slow-motion, sometimes with pretty stupid moves.'

The climbers now want the game to be registered in *The Guinness Book of World Records* as the highest-ever played game of chess. They have the proof, as an American climber made a video of the summit blitz chess duel and can testify to it.

The Return of the Queen

The Walt Disney Studios have released the trailer of *Queen of Katwe,* the movie of the inspiring and upbeat story of 14-year-old Phiona Mutesi, who through chess managed to escape with her family out of their impoverished Katwe slum in Kampala, Uganda. Her life changed when she was captivated by a chance chess lesson being given to children by coach Robert Katande.

The movie is based on Tim Crothers' book of the same name and stars Golden Globe winner David Oyelowo (Katande), Oscar-winner Lupita Nyong'o (Phiona's mother)

David Oyelowo and Madina Nalwanga star in Queen of Katwe.

and newcomer Madina Nalwanga (Phiona). *Queen of Katwe* will open in US theatres on September 23 – and it could see a red carpet return to the US for the premier for Phiona.

In 2014 Phiona was invited to give a talk at the Bill and Melinda Gates Foundation. While in Seattle, the Gates Foundation arranged for her to meet with local educational non-profit, America's Foundation for Chess, and the pioneering work they are doing in US schools. Their First Move programme is now taught to over 150,000 US school children.

And if Phiona does attend the US premiere of Disney's *Queen of Katwe*, already we are hearing rumours that First Move would look favourably to inviting her back to visit some more schools to tell of her inspiring story of how the game of chess lifted her and her family's life; and how in the process it has now helped her to achieve another unlikely goal, that of going to university.

Bobby, Bruce & Bam

If there were a category at the annual chess publishing awards for the most unusual book of the year, then we may have already found the runaway winner with the recent release of *Bobby, Bruce & Bam – The Secrets of Hip-Hop Chess* by Adisa, The Bishop.

Adisa Banjoko, aka The Bishop, is a respected disruptor in the space of education innovation. For years he was promoting the fusion between chess, hip-hop and martial arts while fostering positivity and awareness to help inner-city kids shift their focus to education, entrepreneurship, and life's possibilities. When in 2006, he visited incarcerated youths in San Francisco, this directly led to the formation of the Hip-Hop Chess Federation (HHCF).

Adisa's new tome *Bobby, Bruce & Bam* was a decade in the making, and in it he outlines how the rise in US popular consciousness through the early 1970s of Bobby Fischer,

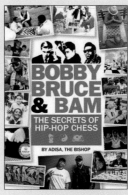
The Bishop reveals the secrets of hip-hop chess.

Bruce Lee and Afrika Bambaataa (the stage name of Kevin Donovan, a controversial American DJ from the South Bronx, who pioneered hip-hop music) influenced America in unexpected ways.

In doing so in the book, the author attempts to find HHCF's guiding philosophy that chess, martial arts and hip-hop can promote unity and non-violence among inner-city kids who might otherwise turn to anti-social behaviour and crime.

In the Pink

Like buses, Disney chess-themed movies seem to arrive in two's these days with their latest being *Alice Through the Looking Glass*, which will be released

Alecia Moore in red.

in US theatres at the end of May. The theme song of the movie, *Just Like Fire*, is sung by the artist formerly known by her colourful stage name of Pink, who has now reverted back to her real name Alecia Moore.

In the video, the hippie chic hitmaker is swinging from a trapeze, falls into a dream world as she crashes through a mirror, where she then goes on to become involved in a prolonged human chess match, which is the main theme of the video.

Readers of Lewis Carroll's surreal fantasies with a girl called Alice may remember that *Through the Looking Glass* has chess running through the fabric of his classic children's book. In a human chess game, Alice becomes a pawn who crosses the board and ends the game after she reaches the

eighth rank. We're happy to discover that also in this new Disney steampunk adventure with Alice (starring Mia Wasikowska in the title role with Johnny Depp as 'The Mad Hatter'), the human chess game plays a very enjoyable part.

Star turn

Nona Gaprindashvili was without a doubt the most dominant Women's World Champion ever, having held the title from 1962-1978. Born in 1941, Nona was the first lady to play in GM events and emerge with a creditable score.

In 1978 she became the first woman to be awarded the grandmaster title, as a result of winning Lone Pine 1977 against a field of 45 players, mostly grandmasters. This was in the decade before the rise of the Polgar sisters, and her performance was such a spectacular result that FIDE thought fit to bend their technical requirements to give her the title outright.

Last year, Georgia's President Giorgi Margvelashvili awarded the five-time former World Champion the country's Order of Excellence. Now we learn another state title has been bestowed on her, that of Cavalier of Sport, to honour her distinguished career. It was presented to her by Prime Minister Giorgi Kvirikashvili at an award ceremony on 3 May to coincide with Nona's 75th birthday. At the same time, a special Star bearing her name was unveiled in the yard of Tbilisi's Chess Palace, which is also named after her.

Nona Gaprindashvili in 1975.

Star Wars

A long time ago, in a galaxy far, far away, there was a futuristic chess battle in the original *Star Wars: Episode IV – A New Hope*. It was the scene where Luke Skywalker is getting to grips with his first light sabre, while the very hirsute Chewbacca and R2-D2 are playing 'battle chess' with monsters. In a conversation with Han Solo and C-3PO, R2-D2 is wisely advised to 'Let the Wookie win'.

That scene involved a specially designed holographic chess set that we thought was the exclusive preserve of the Hollywood special effects department. But not so, it

'Oh well, if that's how you hope to win.'

seems, as now, forty years on, fiction could well become a reality. Phil Tippett, the legendary FX designer who was charged by George Lucas to create that iconic holographic chess set for the Star Wars franchise, has announced that he is launching an actual reality version of it on Kickstart.

Tippett is looking for $100,000 to get the venture going, and he's partnering with veterans of LucasArts video game studio to develop HoloGrid: Monster Battle, based on the holographic chess game from the Star Wars universe. In addition to appearing in the original film, holo-chess has popped up in novelizations, video game adaptations, and again in last year's series reboot *Star Wars: The Force Awakens*. ∎

Fabiano Caruana

As a very little boy of about 9 Fabiano attended the Nassau Chess Club in Mineola, New York, which Harold Stenzl has been effectively running for nearly 40 years. Meeting in a cold church basement, it still gets about 40 attendees every Monday night. It is not far from my home and as an expert it was obvious that Fabiano was a prodigy of some kind. It was also clear to me that he didn't receive the special attention that he deserved, but that could be the subject of another letter / article.

Regarding his notes in New In Chess 2016/2 to his game vs. van Wely, move 24.♗xe7?!

I would like to make a few points:

1) I have a heuristic that I teach my students – never develop your opponents' pieces. That is the drawback of this move. It effectively improves the position of the black king.

2) Then on move 34...♗c8 he states: 'I was expecting 34...♕b6 35.g8♕ ♖xb4+ with a long sequence to follow that he was "worried about"...'

To me this shows too much dependence on computer type analysis. Why not follow your intuition with 35.b5+ as in the game and I think there will be a quick end? Or am I missing something that I should be checking with Fritz which gives Black decisive or frightening counterplay?

Anyway, overall I would like to commend Fabiano's notes to the game – they lend great insight into his thinking and into how one of the world's top few players rated over 2800 today thinks.

I would also like to state that his notes to moves 13-19 show how chess has changed over the past 20 years or so with addition of strong computer analysis. It has become common to castle queenside for White in the English Attack and play b3 (weakening a3 and c3 with confidence that the white king will be safe in the ensuing middlegame, and in fact White will be able to play positionally right in front

Write to us
New In Chess, P.O. Box 1093
1810 KB Alkmaar, The Netherlands
or e-mail: editors@newinchess.com
Letters may be edited or abridged

of his king, exploiting squares like c4 and c5, which 40 years ago we would have never considered because of the obvious danger to the white king. This is an attestment to advances in the game with the help of computer analysis and human theory. I am not saying I wasn't aware of this before Fabiano's notes, but they give further credence to this advancement in the game.

IM Dr. Danny Kopec
Merrick, New York

Rook and Bishop vs. Rook

I agree with your Honorary Editor Jan Timman when he wrote in New In Chess 2016/1 that 'the number of games lost in the rook + bishop vs rook ending, even at grandmaster level, is astounding'. This may be the reason why a senior GM who is also a FIDE Senior Trainer first tested the skills of a high 2600+ GM in this ending when I arranged a few training sessions over Skype for the latter in 2011. A quick look at Mega Database 2016 shows that there are 2942 games with this ending in the database, out of which 273 games were played between players who were both rated 2500 or higher. More than 32% of these 273 games were lost! The importance of knowing this ending was demonstrated in the 2016

Candidates Tournament. Caruana was leading jointly with Karjakin after Round 12 and reached this ending against Svidler in Round 13. The game should have been drawn with perfect play, but Svidler misplayed it on move 102 and Caruana could have won within the 50-move rule, but he too misplayed it on move 105, thereby throwing away the win. Had Caruana won this game he would have needed just a draw against Karjakin in the final round to emerge the challenger to Carlsen for the World Championship Match. The fact that elite players like Caruana and Svidler couldn't play this ending correctly reminds me of Mark Dvoretsky pointing out, 'My work with grandmasters, some of them belonging to the world's Top Ten, have convinced me that almost none of them had studied chess endings systematically' (*Dvoretsky's Endgame Manual*, 2008, p 8).

Uday Bajracharya
Sydney, Australia

COLOPHON

PUBLISHER: Allard Hoogland
EDITOR-IN-CHIEF:
Dirk Jan ten Geuzendam
HONORARY EDITOR:
Jan Timman
CONTRIBUTING EDITOR: Anish Giri
EDITORS: Peter Boel, René Olthof
ART-DIRECTION: Jan Scholtus
PRODUCTION: Joop de Groot
TRANSLATORS: Ken Neat, Piet Verhagen
SALES AND ADVERTISING: Remmelt Otten

© No part of this magazine may be reproduced, stored in a retrieval system or transmitted in any form or by any means, recording or otherwise, without the prior permission of the publisher.

NEW IN CHESS
P.O. BOX 1093
1810 KB ALKMAAR
THE NETHERLANDS

PHONE: 00-31-(0)72-51 27 137
FAX: 00-31-(0)72-51 58 234
E-MAIL:
SUBSCRIPTIONS: nic@newinchess.com
EDITORS: editors@newinchess.com
SALES AND ADVERTISING:
otten@newinchess.com

BANK DETAILS:
IBAN: NL41ABNA 0589126024
BIC: ABNANL2A in favour of Interchess BV, Alkmaar, The Netherlands

WWW.NEWINCHESS.COM

Experts at Classic Chess, but not necessarily at Blitz

It is often said that regular or classic chess, in which players have about two hours to play 40 moves, and blitz chess are almost two different games. To non-chess players, that can be puzzling -- after all, they are the same games, just at different speeds. But in regular chess, players have enough time to calculate so that they can really explore positions and not be caught off-guard. In blitz chess, where there is little or no time to calculate, players react by instinct. Generally, players who are better at tactics excel at faster speeds. The difference between players «regular» chess ability and

blitz strength can be substantial, as can be seen in the following graphic. It shows the top 40 players in the world in regular chess in the May rankings and their corresponding ratings in blitz chess. The ranking also includes Garry Kasparov, who is, of course, a special case as he retired from competition in 2005, so it is difficult to know what his true playing strength might be now. But he did play in the Ultimate Blitz Challenge after the recent United States Championship and accredited himself pretty well.

DYLAN LOEB McCLAIN

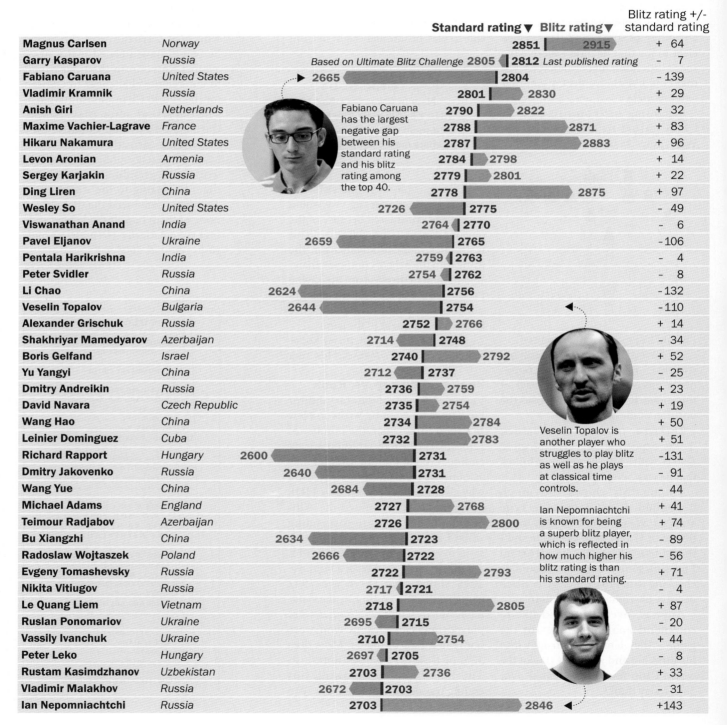

		Standard rating ▼	Blitz rating ▼	Blitz rating +/- standard rating
Magnus Carlsen	Norway	2851	2915	+ 64
Garry Kasparov	Russia	Based on Ultimate Blitz Challenge 2805	2812 Last published rating	− 7
Fabiano Caruana	United States	2665	2804	− 139
Vladimir Kramnik	Russia	2801	2830	+ 29
Anish Giri	Netherlands	2790	2822	+ 32
Maxime Vachier-Lagrave	France	2788	2871	+ 83
Hikaru Nakamura	United States	2787	2883	+ 96
Levon Aronian	Armenia	2784	2798	+ 14
Sergey Karjakin	Russia	2779	2801	+ 22
Ding Liren	China	2778	2875	+ 97
Wesley So	United States	2726	2775	− 49
Viswanathan Anand	India	2764	2770	− 6
Pavel Eljanov	Ukraine	2659	2765	−106
Pentala Harikrishna	India	2759	2763	− 4
Peter Svidler	Russia	2754	2762	− 8
Li Chao	China	2624	2756	−132
Veselin Topalov	Bulgaria	2644	2754	−110
Alexander Grischuk	Russia	2752	2766	+ 14
Shakhriyar Mamedyarov	Azerbaijan	2714	2748	− 34
Boris Gelfand	Israel	2740	2792	+ 52
Yu Yangyi	China	2712	2737	− 25
Dmitry Andreikin	Russia	2736	2759	+ 23
David Navara	Czech Republic	2735	2754	+ 19
Wang Hao	China	2734	2784	+ 50
Leinier Dominguez	Cuba	2732	2783	+ 51
Richard Rapport	Hungary	2600	2731	−131
Dmitry Jakovenko	Russia	2640	2731	− 91
Wang Yue	China	2684	2728	− 44
Michael Adams	England	2727	2768	+ 41
Teimour Radjabov	Azerbaijan	2726	2800	+ 74
Bu Xiangzhi	China	2634	2723	− 89
Radoslaw Wojtaszek	Poland	2666	2722	− 56
Evgeny Tomashevsky	Russia	2722	2793	+ 71
Nikita Vitiugov	Russia	2717	2721	− 4
Le Quang Liem	Vietnam	2718	2805	+ 87
Ruslan Ponomariov	Ukraine	2695	2715	− 20
Vassily Ivanchuk	Ukraine	2710	2754	+ 44
Peter Leko	Hungary	2697	2705	− 8
Rustam Kasimdzhanov	Uzbekistan	2703	2736	+ 33
Vladimir Malakhov	Russia	2672	2703	− 31
Ian Nepomniachtchi	Russia	2703	2846	+143

Fabiano Caruana has the largest negative gap between his standard rating and his blitz rating among the top 40.

Veselin Topalov is another player who struggles to play blitz as well as he plays at classical time controls.

Ian Nepomniachtchi is known for being a superb blitz player, which is reflected in how much higher his blitz rating is than his standard rating.

Bjork: 'When I was 18, science, physics, and math were my favourite. I was a bit of a nerd – the only girl with a lot of boys at chess championships.'

Seth Meyers: 'A woman named Nazi yesterday won the 2016 US Chess Championship. Apparently she claimed the title when a woman named France just gave up.'
(Instant fame for Nazi Paikidze, the new US Women's Champion, as she found herself being the butt of a Seth Meyers joke on his Late Night show following her surprise victory)

Nazi Paikidze: 'Any press is good press!'
(Her tweeted response to Seth Meyers' joke)

Carissa Yip: 'I just want to play chess, nothing else.'
(So says the youngest player – 12 years old – to have competed in the US Chess Championships; scoring a creditable 4½/11 that included a win over defending multi-time champion Irina Krush)

Maurice Ashley: 'I was transported to this world, and I wanted to be one of the grandmasters.'
(On recently becoming the first black player inducted into the US Chess Hall of Fame)

Frank Herbert:
'Logic is good for playing chess but is often too slow for the needs of survival.'
(The American sci-fi writer, famous for his novel Dune)

Tyrion Lannister: 'I hope Your Grace will pardon me. Your king is trapped. Death in four.'
(Playing Cyvasse in Game of Thrones)

Vladimir Makagonov: 'When no other obvious plan is available, just try to improve your worst piece.'
(Words of wisdom from Vasily Smyslov's trainer)

Vasily Smyslov: 'In chess, as in life, a man is his own most dangerous opponent.'

Stefan Zweig: 'In chess, as a purely intellectual game, where randomness is excluded, for someone to play against himself is absurd... it is as paradoxical as attempting to jump over his own shadow.'

Isaac Bashevis Singer: 'We all play chess with Fate as partner. He makes a move, we make a move. He tries to checkmate us in three moves, we try to prevent it. We know we can't win, but we're driven to give him a good fight.'
(From the Nobel Prize-winner's The Collected Stories of Isaac Bashevis Singer)

George RR Martin: 'A bit of chess, a bit of blitzkrieg, a bit of Stratego. Mix well and add imagination.'
(The chess-loving Game of Thrones author, on how he created Cyvasse, the chess-equivalent played in the cult fantasy series)

Lev Alburt: 'A month later I traveled on to John F. Kennedy airport. All my belongings easily fit into a small bag; I had $80 in my pocket. I had to win tournaments to make a decent living. Soon, I was the No 1-ranked US chess player.'
(In a Guardian feature 'I was a Soviet defector. Chess was my door to freedom', describing the moment in 1979 when he left West Germany for his new life in America)

Arnold Schwarzenegger: 'There is nothing like chess to keep the brain smart, and give it a workout.'

Anatoly Karpov: 'One who has never seen a game of chess is, in my opinion, an unhappy person.'

Arturo Perez-Reverte: 'Chess is all about getting the king into check, you see. It's about killing the father. I would say that chess has more to do with the art of murder than it does with the art of war.'
(The Spanish award-winning novelist in his chess-themed mystery novel The Flanders Panel)

Magnus Carlsen, together with Hans Olav Lahlum and Jon-Ludvig Hammer, in the studio of TV2, the Norwegian TV channel that broadcast the games live.

(Below) The trademark Norway Chess Mini Coopers lined up in front of the Stavanger Konserthus, where the last three rounds were played.

It is his tournament, but year after year it eluded him. What was keeping him from winning the star event in his home country? That question belongs to the past. In his fourth attempt, Magnus Carlsen knew no doubts. Not even a slip in the penultimate round could

JOACHIM STEINBRU

undermine his determination, and when he hit back on the final day, he claimed Altibox Norway Chess 2016. **DIRK JAN TEN GEUZENDAM** reports from Stavanger.

Fourth time lucky for Magnus Carlsen

At first I figured that the Norway Chess organizers had set the starting time of the rounds at 4 p.m. to accommodate their star Magnus Carlsen, who is a notorious late riser. But the explanation was more prosaic. They started late in the afternoon at the request of TV2, who were going to broadcast the tournament live on Norwegian television and were hoping to show the most exciting moments of the games in prime time. With the slightly faster time-control (40 moves in 100 minutes, then 20/50, then 15 minutes plus 30-second increments from move 60), this proved to be a wise choice. On most days, Carlsen's games finished before 8 p.m., and once he had paid his visit to their studio, the TV2 people could pack up for the day, as few Norwegian viewers would continue to follow the other games anyway.

However, starting at four did have an unexpected drawback for the foreign guests. As many Norwegians finish work between 3 and 4 p.m., the players' transfer from their hotel to the venue took place during the rush hour! As a result, the caravan of 10 Mini Coopers, which has become a Norway Chess trademark, had to leave quite early to bridge only a short distance. The only player not affected by this early departure was Carlsen, who cleverly exploited another Norwegian peculiarity. In environment-conscious Norway, a fast lane that can only be used by buses and electronic cars runs beside the normal lanes, so Henrik Carlsen would rush his son past the slow traffic in the latter's Tesla and drop him off as close as possible to the playing hall, where Magnus would get into his Mini Cooper and arrive to face the waiting photographers and television cameras like all the rest.

Carlsen's small privileges and occasional prima donna behaviour didn't ruffle any feathers. That there were two fridges in the players' rest room, one with his name on it and one plain one, merely brought a smile to some of his colleagues' faces. And that he lacked the patience to wait for his turn to appear on the international broadcast a couple of times was just a pity, because every time he did join commentators Jan Gustafsson and Peter Svidler, it was invariably one of the highlights of the day.

But when all's said and done, everyone understands and appreciates that without Carlsen there just would not be a Norway Chess tournament. Ever since its start in 2013, the event has been built around the World Champion. He is the first player to be invited and the plan is that he faces world-class opposition to make Norway Chess one of the elite events on the calendar.

This was a bit more complicated this time. To begin with, Norway Chess's decision to leave the Grand Chess Tour after its first experiences with this tournament cycle definitely affected the line-up. The philosophy of the team in Stavanger has always been that they want to stage an event that supports itself with sponsorship money and television deals. This idea had begun to clash increasingly with the approach of the Sinquefield Cup and the London Classic, both of which heavily depend on the generosity of rich chess-loving individuals. As Norway Chess and the Grand Chess Tour parted ways, both sides issued amicable press releases wishing the others well, but it was clear that not everyone was happy. Barely had Norway Chess publicly announced their decision, or the dates of the US Championships in St. Louis were revealed, which happened to clash with the tournament in Stavanger. The organizers in St. Louis called it an unfortunate coincidence, saying they had not found alternative dates for the championship, but it would probably be hard to find someone in Norway who believed that.

The clash was also unfortunate for the three favourites in St. Louis – Caruana, Nakamura and So – who were essentially robbed of the opportunity to play in an elite event, as everyone understood that it wouldn't be wise for any of them to decline to play in their national championship.

The problems for the Norwegians didn't end there. Less than two weeks before the first round, Sergey Karjakin informed them that he was too exhausted after the Candidates' tournament in Moscow. Obviously everyone wanted to see the Russian in action, now that he had won the right to challenge Carlsen for the world title, and he had signed the contract, but what can you do if a player really doesn't want to play? In the end, the organizers started negotiations with Karjakin to find a way for him to

'Both sides issued amicable press releases wishing the others well, but it was clear that not everyone was happy.'

compensate them (think of a simul or another exhibition in Norway) and decided to invite a last-minute replacement.

Still, you wouldn't guess that the Norwegians would have had such headaches if you looked at the fine field they put together in the end. With five players from the world's Top-10 and five grandmasters that are clearly on the rise and deserve a broader audience, Altibox Norway Chess offered a delightful and delectable mix.

It's always great to see 'new' faces in elite events, and here there were quite a few to watch with particular interest. Pentala Harikrishna was one of them. He is the current Number Two in India and Number 13 in the world. The gap between him and India's leading player, Vishy Anand,

is smaller than ever, and in January Harikrishna even briefly surpassed the former World Champion in the live ratings. This attracted worldwide attention, but it didn't overly excite the 29-year-old grandmaster from Hyderabad. He prefers to look at his own achievements rather than compare himself to others. Yet it's true that he has been doing quite well lately. Ever since he moved to Belgrade a little over a year ago to be closer to the action in Europe, he has gained more than 30 points, and this progress seems to herald a new phase in his already long career. Just imagine, Harikrishna became U-10 Junior World Champion 20 years ago, and a grandmaster at the age of 15 in 2001, even before the big chess boom in India.

'Hari' finished shared sixth and said he took home good feelings from Norway. 'After Wijk aan Zee (2014), it had been a long time since my last super-tournament. It's nice to play against so many strong players at once. Playing against one really strong player in a tournament and playing them every day are two very different things. The games were quite interesting. I had four decisive games, two wins and two losses. Against Magnus and Kramnik I didn't play my best, but I also have to give credit to them; they played better than me. There is always scope for improvement.'

Harikrishna collected the same number of points as his good friend Li Chao, who was the last-minute substitute for Karjakin. Although he is China's number two player by rating, Li Chao, who turned 27 on the day of Round 3, is less well-known than the players that won gold for their country at the Olympiad and the World Teams. Due to a conflict with the Chinese federation that he prefers not to speak about, he is not eligible for the national team. His sharp rise in the world rankings is mainly due to the Open tournaments he has played in Europe. Small wonder, then, that he was delighted to receive an invi-

Li Chao postponed one of his wedding parties to come to Stavanger as a last-minute replacement for Sergey Karjakin.

JOACHIM STEINBRU

tation to Norway Chess, except for one thing... Last year he got married and getting married in China is not something you do in one day. Once you have tied the knot, you are expected to arrange several wedding parties; in his case one in his native city, Taiyuan, one in his wife's birthplace and one in the city where he is living now, Changzhou, the 'Panda City', where he runs a chess school with GM Wang Yue. The first wedding party had been scheduled for the last weekend of Norway Chess. In the beginning he hoped he might be able to fly back immediately after the last game and still be in time, but he soon realized that this was unrealistic. Fortunately, both his father and his wife Hou Bin ('She understands everything. I was so lucky to find her.') persuaded him to postpone the party and go to Stavanger.

Before the tournament he said that he believed that his 2755 rating was too high and that 2710 or 2720 was a better indication of his strength, but his performance rating turned out to be 2771 – perhaps because he largely remained true to his active style of play, of which he had said that it was more suited to Open tournaments and might cause problems against the very best.

One of the players to find out how inventive and tenacious Li can be was Nils Grandelius, who failed to convert a huge advantage. The Swedish GM's rating was more than 100 points below that of the 'second-weakest' participant, but he refused to feel any fear, and although he did end in last place, the 22-year-old from Lund enjoyed the tournament from the first game to the last. As part of his preparation he had had a special training session with his coach Evgeny Agrest, who had given him an original task. He told him to study the losses of his far stronger opponents, not only to find their weaknesses, but mainly to understand that they, too, are humans with occasional weak moments.

The blitz loss to an 'unusually aggressive' Anish Giri didn't really affect the World Champion's play, as he burst away to take an early lead in the main tournament.

But no matter how interesting the 'new faces' were, in the end it was all about Magnus Carlsen, of course. The World Champion had won his last three tournaments and there was no question that he was burning to add a fourth victory. The first signs were encouraging. In the blitz tournament that served to draw lots, he scored 7½ points from his first 8 games with dominating and seemingly effortless play. The fly in the ointment was the 9th and last game, which he lost to Anish Giri, who was also playing great blitz.

Carlsen won the blitz anyway and chose number 5, which gives the ideal pairings, and remained in a good mood as he tweeted: 'Very happy with my play in Norway Chess blitz today, despite failing to put up any resistance against an unusually aggressive Anish Giri.'

RL 7.1 – C65
Anish Giri
Magnus Carlsen
Stavanger blitz 2016 (9)
1.e4 e5 2.♘f3 ♘c6 3.♗b5 ♘f6 4.d3 ♗c5 5.♗xc6 dxc6 6.♘bd2 ♗e6 7.0-0 ♘d7 8.♘b3 ♗b6 9.♘g5 ♗xb3 10.axb3

10...♕e7 A new plan to go ...0-0-0, which doesn't work in this game. In the same blitz tournament, Giri-Kramnik saw 10...f6 11.♘f3 ♘c5 12.♘d2 0-0 (½ -½, 58). **11.♗d2 0-0-0** According to plan, but... **12.b4!**

Black is too late to save the bishop from being buried. He tries, only to make things even worse.

12...♔b8 The position after 12...f6 13.♘f3 ♘f8 14.c4 a6 15.c5 ♗a7 16.♗e3 does look pleasant for White. **13.c4 ♗d4** Black is persisting and clearly isn't happy with 13...f6 14.♘f3 a6 15.c5 ♗a7 either. **14.♘f3** This gives White a clear advantage, as Black cannot really take on b2. **14...♘f8 15.♕a4** White's initiative on the queenside makes Black's life very difficult. **15...a6 16.b5** Winning a pawn. **16...cxb5 17.cxb5 ♕d7 18.bxa6 ♕xa4 19.♖xa4 ♘e6 20.axb7 ♘c5** 20...♔xb7 also leaves White in the driver's seat. **21.♖a3!**

21...♗xb2 22.♖a2! Winning a piece and much stronger than 22.♖a8+ ♔xb7 23.♖xd8 ♖xd8 24.♖b1 ♘a4! 25.♗c1 ♖xd3 26.♗xb2 ♖b3. **22...♘xd3 23.♖b1** And as he let his clock count down to 0.00,

Carlsen blitzed out **23...c5**, losing on time. After 24.♘e1, White would win anyway.

For Giri the blitz tournament also seemed to point at excellent form, particularly when he won his first game against Pavel Eljanov the following day. But he suffered a serious blow in the second round, when he came up with a strong idea in a sharp Najdorf, only to be out-tricked by Maxime Vachier-Lagrave. When Giri missed the point of the Frenchman's reply, he was suddenly confronted by a strong central break that gave Black a dream position, soon followed by a winning attack.

Uncharacteristically, the Dutchman also lost a second game with White in Round 6, when Harikrishna countered excellently from a French Defence. Giri kept trying, but in the end he had to settle for a disappointing 8th place.

In the meantime, Carlsen seemed to have taken a firm grip on the tournament. After six rounds he was leading with four points, half a point ahead of a group of four players and half a point more than the total he collected last year. He also equalled a personal record, as he had once again gone without defeat in 41 games. He

broke that record in the next round when he fulfilled a wish he had expressed on the eve of the tournament: to beat Vladimir Kramnik. But it wasn't one of their great fights. A new idea found by Jon-Ludvig Hammer gave Carlsen a promising position, and when Kramnik failed to solve his problems, the game was essentially over before 20 moves had been played. As Kramnik summed it up, 'That was just bad luck. It happens very rarely these days that you essentially close a line that had been played for dozens of years. It was regarded as solid, and now you cannot play it anymore. Once I saw ♘e2, which for me is definitely the novelty of the year, I knew I had a choice between a very unpleasant endgame, which is especially unpleasant against him, and going for some concrete play in the hope it would work, but I lost without a fight.'

QO 11.4 – D35
Magnus Carlsen
Vladimir Kramnik
Stavanger 2016 (7)

1.d4 d5 2.c4 e6 3.♘c3 ♘f6 4.cxd5 exd5 5.♗g5 c6 6.e3 ♗f5 Nigel Short's move. **7.♕f3 ♗g6 8.♗xf6 ♕xf6 9.♕xf6 gxf6 10.♘f3 ♘d7 11.♘h4 ♗e7**

12.♘e2 The usual move here is 12.g3, but this is a venomous new idea found by Carlsen's second Jon-Ludvig Hammer. **12...♘b6 13.♘g3 ♗b4+ 14.♔d1 ♘a4?**

A bad move that gives White a free hand to demonstrate his idea. Kramnik started looking for an alternative when he saw that after 14...♘c8 15.♘gf5 ♗d6 16.♗d3 Black cannot kick out the knight on f5 to create counterplay; a highly frustrating prospect.

15.♘gf5 ♔d7

Here, or on any of the subsequent moves, he should have withdrawn the knight with 15...♘b6. After the game Kramnik opined that instead of 15...♘b6, which promises little, he could have tried 15...♘xb2+ 16.♔c2 ♘c4 17.♗xc4 dxc4 18.♖hb1 c5 19.a3 ♗a5 20.♘xg6 hxg6 21.♘d6+ ♔d7 22.♘xb7 ♗b6 23.dxc5 ♗c7 24.h3, and now for instance 24...♔c6 25.♘d6, which would have left him with an uphill struggle but with a decidedly better position than in the game.

16.♖b1 A strong move also missed by Kramnik.

16...♔e6 17.♗d3 ♖hc8 18.♔e2

18...♗f8 Here he had been hoping to play 18...c5... until he saw 19.a3 ♗a5 20.dxc5 ♘xc5 21.♘d4+, followed by ♗xg6 and b4, and White wins.

19.g4

And as Kramnik summed it up: 'This is just lost; the rest is not interesting.'

19...c5 Looking for counterplay, but it doesn't work at all. Carlsen: 'It just makes the position a lot worse without offering counterchances.' **20.♘g2 cxd4 21.exd4 ♗d6** For understandable reasons Kramnik didn't want to resign, but the rest of the game no longer required anything special from Carlsen. **22.h4 h5 23.♘g7+ ♔e7 24.gxh5 ♗xd3+ 25.♔xd3 ♔d7 26.♘e3 ♘b6 27.♘g4 ♖h8 28.♖he1 ♗e7 29.♘f5 ♗d8 30.h6 ♖c8 31.b3 ♖c6 32.♘ge3 ♗c7 33.♖bc1 ♖xc1 34.♖xc1 ♗f4 35.♖c5 ♔e6 36.♘g7+ ♔d6 37.♘g4 ♘d7 38.♖c2** The rook is heading for the e-file. **38...f5 39.♘xf5+ ♔e6 40.♘g7+ ♔d6 41.♖e2 ♔c6 42.♖e8 ♖xe8 43.♘xe8 ♘f8 44.♘e5+ ♗xe5 45.dxe5 ♔d7 46.♘f6+ ♔e6 47.h5 ♔xe5 48.♘d7+ ♘xd7 49.h7 ♘c5+ 50.♔e2** Black resigned.

Everything seemed decided, but then it was Magnus Carlsen who had a poor day, and Levon Aronian who took full advantage to score a sweet

Magnus Carlsen had expressed his hope to beat Vladimir Kramnik, but he could not have expected that it would be so easy. Kramnik called the Norwegian's 12th move 'definitely the novelty of the year'.

victory. The Armenian had been lying in wait with a string of draws in the first six rounds and then scored his first win against Eljanov. And now he had caught up with Carlsen, and with one round to go they were in a group of seven players who could theoretically still win first prize.

But one way or another it didn't feel that way, because Carlsen was to play Eljanov, who had just lost two games, as White, and Aronian was playing Harikrishna with Black. If Aronian drew and Carlsen won, it didn't matter what happened in the other games. And that is what happened on the last day. Aronian was better against Harikrishna, but let his advantage slip, and Carlsen struck mercilessly when Eljanov succumbed to the pressure in a position that a computer would probably have saved.

Carlsen's victory was welcomed with great relief and joy. It isn't often that you see young chess fans coming out of the playing room shouting and cheering, celebrating the victory of their hero. Carlsen himself was delighted too, of course, but he was also his own severest critic: 'I didn't play any good games. There were some interesting games and I definitely enjoyed playing some of them, but I didn't like the end result of my work.' Only to add: 'But they were good enough.'

Everybody happy

Interestingly, his main competitors preferred to stress the good sides of their performances and barely expressed any frustration, in a way confirming how deserved Carlsen's win had been. Just listen to them as they express their feelings about their performance in Norway.

Aronian: 'It was good as a comeback after a difficult Candidates tournament. After Moscow I didn't leave my apartment for a week. I felt ashamed, actually, because I had played so badly. And I could have done better. And people in Armenia love chess and I didn't feel comfort-

able about facing them. It was good to go to Norway, far away from big cities. It was a good opportunity and a good place to recover. I think that my game against Magnus was important psychologically. I am very happy

> '**After Moscow I didn't leave my apartment for a week. I felt ashamed, actually, because I had played so badly.**'

with that game. In the last round I didn't use my chances and I hadn't expected Eljanov to lose so quickly. I was upset about that a bit. But it was still a good tournament.'

Vachier-Lagrave: 'I finished one point behind Magnus, so I was never really close. But of course, if I had managed to score in the games in which I definitely had chances – against Pavel Eljanov, against Magnus, maybe against Vladimir, and of course against Nils at the end... That's a lot of missed chances, but if you miss them you cannot count on winning the tournament. Of course it would have been

better to have won these games, but it's not something you can complain about because no one is responsible for these misses except I myself. I really felt I was a serious contender, which probably changed after I had played Magnus. I put him under serious pressure, but I basically let him escape. Of late my first objective had been to stabilize in the Top-10, but the Top 5-is more exciting, of course, and it also shows that I am a serious contender to at least play in the Candidates' and maybe win it next time.'

Topalov: 'Let's say I played quite a decent tournament, very professional and serious from the beginning. But as always I had five black games because of my blitz skills. And except against Vachier, I had absolutely no chance to win any of my black games. I won against Nils, of course, and my second chance to win was against Vachier. That would have given me a chance to play for the tournament, but I blew it. But in general I am quite happy.'

Kramnik: 'All in all, I am quite satisfied, because my level of play was fine, especially because I always have problems playing after a long break. It had been, like, two months, and I always need time to get into competitive shape. The result is OK, nothing special. And my play was fine; no more, no less, just fine for my level. I might have scored half a point more, perhaps, but it was fine. It was not a great tournament for me, but it was not a failure either.'

Stavanger 2016				1	2	3	4	5	6	7	8	9	10		cat. XXI TPR
1 **Magnus Carlsen**	IGM	NOR	2851	*	0	½	½	1	½	1	½	1	1	6	2886
2 **Levon Aronian**	IGM	ARM	2784	1	*	½	½	½	½	½	½	1	½	5½	2848
3 **Maxime Vachier-Lagrave**	IGM	FRA	2788	½	½	*	½	½	½	½	1	½	½	5	2811
4 **Veselin Topalov**	IGM	BUL	2754	½	½	½	*	½	½	½	½	½	1	5	2814
5 **Vladimir Kramnik**	IGM	RUS	2801	0	½	½	½	*	½	1	½	½	1	5	2809
6 **Li Chao**	IGM	CHN	2755	½	½	½	½	½	*	0	½	1	½	4½	2771
7 **Pentala Harikrishna**	IGM	IND	2763	0	½	½	½	0	1	*	1	½	½	4½	2770
8 **Anish Giri**	IGM	NED	2790	½	½	0	½	½	½	0	*	1	½	4	2724
9 **Pavel Eljanov**	IGM	UKR	2765	0	0	½	½	½	0	½	0	*	1	3	2645
10 **Nils Grandelius**	IGM	SWE	2649	0	½	½	0	0	½	½	½	0	*	2½	2617

NOTES BY
Peter Heine Nielsen

SI 43.4 – B29
**Magnus Carlsen
Nils Grandelius**
Stavanger 2016 (3)

Magnus had a good start to Norway Chess, beating Harikrishna in the first round and then drawing a very solidity-minded Topalov. Next was the young Swedish top player Nils Grandelius, who in the qualifier had edged out local favourite Jon-Ludvig Hammer.

Nils announced at the press conference that he was afraid of no-one, and that he would stay loyal to his style. He certainly kept his word, even when facing the World Champion.

1.e4 c5 2.♘f3 ♘f6?!

This is a line the Swedish team had prepared for the 2015 European Championship in Reykjavik, and which Nils used to make a draw against Adams. After the game he was asked when he had made his mistake, and said 'On move two!' It is true that the line is probably dubious, but the decisive mistake came later.

3.e5!

Part of the reason 2...♘f6 is not very popular is that after 3.♘c3 Black's best option is probably just 3...d6, which after 4.d4 transposes back to main line Sicilians, as in Grandelius's recent game against Harikrishna. However, Nils's clever point is this would have avoided Magnus pet line 3.♗b5+. But 3.♘c3 is a kind

of a lazy reaction to 2...♘f6, so one could argue that Nils actually forced Magnus to play the best move!

3...♘d5 4.♘c3

4...♘xc3

4...e6 used to be Black's try years ago, when 5.♘xd5 exd5 6.d4 ♘c6 7.dxc5 ♗xc5 8.♕xd5 ♕b6 9.♗c4! leads to complications favourable for White, causing black players to abandon the line.

5.dxc3 ♘c6 6.♗f4 ♕b6!?

This, however, is Black's new idea, resurrecting the line. Black used to play a set-up with the queen on c7 followed by castling queenside, but then White can develop easily with ♗d3, ♕e2, 0-0-0, etc. Now Black tries to force a weakness. After 7.♖b1, castling queenside is ruled out altogether, while 7.b3 at least gives Black a target on c3 if White were to aim for 0-0-0. All this led Magnus to the conclusion that the correct way to handle the position was:

7.♕c1!?

Of course the queen can be said to be awkwardly placed on c1, but despite the open d-file it was not much use on d1 anyway. And while 0-0-0 has been

postponed at least for the moment, White does have the simple plan of ♗d3 and 0-0, whereas Black will find it much harder to come up with a sensible way to finish his development.

7...f6!?

Nils took his time, and then played this principled move.

Ipatov had tried 7...h6 8.h4 d5, but after 9.exd6 exd6, 10.♕e3+ is an obvious improvement with a pleasant position for White.

Now, however, Black tries to undermine the white centre, intending either the bold ...g5 or ...d6 exd6 e5!.

8.♗c4!?

A logical developing move that makes 8...d6 look less attractive. After 9.exf6 gxf6 10.♕e3!? Black gets a huge centre, but it looks as if White's speedy development is the relevant factor. Black might have to play 10...e5, but then White gets a grip on the light squares in return. Nils shows no fear, and again plays a principled move:

8...g5!?

9.♗g3!?

9.exf6 was a piece sacrifice similar to the game. After 9...gxf4 10.♕xf4 it even seems as if White has gained some time, but the f3-knight is a weaker attacking piece than the g3-bishop. And concretely, after 10...♞a5! there seems to be no efficient follow-up for White.

9...g4

10.exf6!

I praised Nils's courage, but one has to give credit to Magnus's lack of fear too. The piece sacrifice is purely intuitive; he believes White's compensation to be sufficient.

10...gxf3 11.♕f4!?

Played quickly, and very much planned when sacrificing the piece. It aims at both the f7- and c7-squares, hoping to catch the black king in the centre, and not caring about Black getting a tempo by taking on g2. White, however, had an interesting alternative, and while 12... h5! seems to hold after the game continuation, 11.0-0 might actually be very relevant for the theoretical debate about 2...♞f6, should such a thing exist... After 11.0-0,

11...fxg2 12.♖fe1 just helps White, so Black should either go for 11...

e6, when 12.♕f4 looks very dangerous for Black, since 12...♕f7 13.♖ad1 d5? 14.♖xd5! crashes through, or for 11...♞a5!, when 12.f7+ ♚d8 13.♗d5 ♕g6 looks like the critical line, with a strange position in which I think White has at least sufficient compensation for the sacrificed piece.

11...fxg2!?

Greedy and good. After the immediate 11...♞a5, as Magnus pointed out in the post mortem, 12.fxe7 ♗xe7 13.♗f7 ♚f8! would have been an important resource for Black, since he need not fear the discovered check. He is also threatening 14...♕f6, consolidating his position and practically forcing White to go for perpetual check. However, 12.f7+! ♚d8 13.♗d5 gives White great compensation similar to the game.

11...h5 provides White with 0-0 options, negating the point of ...h5, so Black's move order is the correct one.

12.♖g1

12...♞a5?

A very logical move, but possibly the losing mistake! The absolutely only way is 12...h5!, which not only prevents queenside castling due to

...♗h6, but also creates the option of harassing the white bishop with ...h4.

After 13.fxe7 ♗xe7 14.♕f7+ ♚d8 15.♕g7 ♖e8 16.0-0-0 ♞a5 17.♗f7, 17...♕f6! defends just in time, while 14.0-0-0 ♚d8 also seems to hold up fairly well.

Trying to continue along similar lines as in the game with 13.f7+?! ♚d8 14.0-0-0 runs into 14...h4! 15.♗xh4 ♕c7!, when White's attack seems too slow. And 14.♖xg2 d6 15.0-0-0 ♞c7 16.♗h4 ♗g4! also defends well.

Probably best is 13.♖xg2!?, when 13...♚d8! 14.fxe7+ (on 14.0-0-0?! ♗h6 15.♕xh6 ♖xh6 16.♗f4 d6! defends) 14...♗xe7 15.0-0-0 h4 16.♗xh4 ♗xh4 17.♖g8+ ♖xg8 18.♕xh4+ ♚c7 19.♗xg8 leads to an equal position. Black has an extra piece but White's attack and the h-pawn provide compensation.

13.f7+

After 13.fxe7 ♗xe7 14.♗f7+, 14...♚f8! is again strong, forcing White to restrict himself to a draw by perpetual check.

13...♚d8 14.♗d5

One of the key positions in the game.

At first it looks as if Black has survived the worst. His king will be safe on c7, and having 'lured' White's pawn to f7, his e7-d6-c5 construction looks solid. Initially the computers agree, but after a few minutes they come to the realization that White is winning. Grandelius thought for half an hour, but arrived at the same result. Yes, Black's king is safe, but there is no reasonable plan to stop a white rook from invading on g8. 14...d6 15.0-0-0 ♔c7 16.♖xg2 ♗h3 17.♖gg1 is the illustrative main line. After 17...♘c6 he even pauses for 18.♔b1, as 18...♘e5 will then be met by 19.♕h4!, and 18...♗d7 19.♗h4 ♘e5 20.♖g8 ♘g6 21.♕e4 ♗c6 22.c4 leaves Black in a hopeless position, despite his extra piece. Nils decided to sacrifice a rook for some counterplay, but it was not enough.
14...♗h6?! 15.♕e5 ♖f8 16.♗h4!

Considering the awe-inspiring rating gap of 269(!) points, Nils Grandelius deserved praise for his courageous play, but Magnus Carlsen didn't show any fear either.

This is the problem. Mate is threatened on e7, and Black has to give the rook to lure the white bishop away from attacking the c6-square, since if 16...♘c6, 17.♗xc6 ♖xf7 18.♖xg2 wins on the spot.
16...♖xf7 17.♗xf7 ♘c6 18.♕g3 ♕xb2 19.♖d1 ♕xc2 20.♗d5

Materialistically speaking, things are not all that bad for Black, but the white attack makes the overall situation hopeless.
20...♕f5 21.♖xg2 ♗f4 22.♕f3!? 22.♕xf4!? ♕xf4 23.♖g8+ ♔c7 24.♗g3 was simple and strong, but Magnus plays for the maximum.
22...♔c7 23.♖g5 ♕f8

24.♗g3?! After the game he expressed his dissatisfaction with this inaccuracy. Taking on c6 first would have been simpler.
24...e5 25.♖h5?! Actually, 25.♗xc6! was still possible, as Nils intended 25...♕e7!?, which is tactically creative, since it gets him out of the f-file pin and prepares a discov-

ered check on the e-file. However, it falls short after 26.♖h5 dxc6 27.♕e4!, attacking h7 and thus winning comfortably for White.
25...a5 26.♖xh7 ♖a6 27.♗f7 ♕e8 28.♔f1 ♗xg3 29.hxg3 ♕h8 30.♔g2 ♘d8

31.♖f8 ♕g7 32.♖h1 ♖h6 33.♖xh6 ♕xh6 34.♕f6 ♖xf6 35.♖xf6 d6 36.♔f3 b5 37.g4 ♔d7 38.♖h6
And here Grandelius resigned.
Even though the rather dull technical phase at the end dragged out the game a bit, the fireworks right from the start made it an amazing and surprising game for a super-tournament. It also gave Magnus the lead, which he never relinquished.

NOTES BY
Levon Aronian

RE 3.3 – A15
Levon Aronian
Magnus Carlsen
Stavanger 2016 (8)

1.c4

In recent times I have taken a liking to this move. After all, in the main openings too much is already known, and contortions such as 1.d4 and, after any move, 2.♗f4 do not yet attract me. It only remains to rely on the openings of my early youth – the English and the Réti.

1...♘f6 2.g3

A little psychological moment. At this point I was a point behind my opponent, and naturally I was aiming to

> 'I decided to give him freedom of choice, thereby demonstrating that I had come along to the game without placing the accent on the opening.'

play for a win. Sensing that he would most probably expect that I would try to catch him in theoretical snares, and that, as often happens, he would be ready to surprise me in some way, I decided to give him freedom of choice, thereby demonstrating that I had come along to the game without placing the accent on the opening.

2...c6

I suspect that, having been given a choice of at least five different openings, my opponent was surprised, and over the next few moves he was unable to decide what was most to his taste that day. Thinking for long periods, Magnus began using up lots of time, and by the tenth move the difference on the clocks was already appreciable. A great success!

3.♗g2 d5 4.♘f3 g6 5.b3

It did not make sense to play 5.♕a4, since this is the favourite move of Magnus himself in similar positions, which he even once employed against me in the Melody Amber tournament.

5...♗g7 6.♗b2 0-0 7.0-0

One of the tabiyas of the so-called double fianchetto in the Grünfeld Defence. A couple of years ago I did not imagine playing such quiet variations for White, but, as experience shows, to achieve success it is useful to change periodically.

7...dxc4

7...♗g4 8.d3 ♗xf3 9.♗xf3 e6 is often played, with a solid position. The move in the game has been chosen by Grünfeld experts such as Svidler and Gelfand.

8.bxc4 c5

9.d3 After the game Magnus told me he remembered that the strongest move was 9.♘a3 (with the aim of retaining the option of playing d4), but not how to play correctly against 9.d3. Bearing in mind that I was seeing this position for the first time, a subtle move like 9.♘a3 did not occur to me.

9...♘c6 While my opponent was thinking here for a long time, I endeavoured to find other moves for Black apart from 9...♘c6. I decided that 9...♘e8 was the only alternative. After 10.♗xg7 ♘xg7 11.♘g5, although White has a pleasant position, this was possibly the best solution for Black.

10.♘e5 It is surprising, but this natural move, which I made in two seconds, is not one of the first four choices of my computer program. Should I change the program or my brains?

10...♘a5 I also considered this move to be the most correct. There is no way that Black can allow White to exchange on c6, while after the knight exchange on e5 White has an extremely clear plan – place his knight on c3, queen on a4, rook on b1 and not allow Black to develop his queenside.

11.♕c1 Preparing ♘d2-b3 or ♗c3 and ♕a3.

Levon Aronian specifies one of his ideas after he has sensationally defeated Magnus Carlsen and caught up with him in the penultimate round.

11...♕c7

An unexpected move. Apart from the fact that I was anticipating the pleasure of an improved Volga Gambit endgame after 11...♘g4 12.♘xg4 ♗xg4 13.♗xg7 ♔xg7 14.♕f4 ♕d4 15.♕xd4+ cxd4 16.♖e1, I also spent a long time calculating 11...♘d7 12.♘xd7 ♗xb2 13.♕xb2 ♗xd7 14.♘d2 ♘c6 15.♕xb7 ♖b8 16.♕a6 ♖b6 17.♕a4 ♘d4 18.♕d1. According to my calculations, White succeeds in consolidating and retaining his extra pawn.

For the complete picture, I should mention that after the solid but passive 11...♖b8 12.♘d2 ♘g4 13.♘xg4 ♗xg4 14.♗xg7 ♔xg7 15.♘b3 White's position is slightly more pleasant.

12.♘d2 ♘e8 I took this move to be an attempt to justify 11...♕c7. As I learned after the game, my opponent did not yet see anything terrible for him.

13.f4 ♘d6

After 13...f6 14.♘ef3 ♘c6 15.♘b3 b6 16.d4 White has a solid positional advantage, but perhaps Black should have aimed for something like this.

14.♗c3 Of course, White also has a stable advantage after 14.♘b3 ♘xb3 15.axb3 a5, but when one can win a pawn for free I can rarely restrain myself.

14...♖b8 As my opponent described in the press conference, when he played 12...♘e8, in the variation 13.f4 ♘d6 14.♗c3 f6 he overlooked the winning move 15.♕a3.

15.♕a3

The white pieces have performed gloriously and are rewarded with dark chocolate confectionary (a5-c5).

15...b6 16.♗xa5 bxa5 17.♘b3

17...♘b7

After 17...♘f5 and the series of correct moves 18.♕xc5 ♕xc5+ 19.♘xc5 ♖b2 20.♔f2 ♘d4 21.♗f3 White gets rid of the active rook on b2 with ♖fb1 and has good winning chances.

18.♗xb7 I also considered 18.♘c6, but after some thought and remembering my talent for not normally making the most obvious and best moves, I decided on this occasion to be original.

18...♕xb7 After 18...♖xb7 or 18...♗xb7 it is not clear how to avoid the queen exchange after ♕xc5.

19.♘xc5

19...♕c7

I thought that Magnus would play 19...♕b6 and try to muddy the water with two rooks against a queen. As he rightly remarked after the game, it is not essential for White to play subtly in order to win – for example, 20.♖ab1 ♕xb1 21.♖xb1 ♖xb1+ 22.♔f2 ♖h1 23.♘f3 and the queen begins to pick up pawns.

20.d4 Clearly, Black must now act quickly before White reinforces his heroic knights.

20...♖d8

After the strongest 20...f6 21.♘ed3 ♖d8 22.d5 White has a big advantage, but there is still a lot of play in the position. I suspect that as Black I would also have played 20...♖d8, since without attacking e5 it is not clear how to continue.

21.♖fd1 f6

Now, although Black is able to play e5, surprisingly this does not promise him anything good.

22.♘f3 e5 23.fxe5 fxe5 24.♘xe5

24...♗xe5 After 24...♖xd4 25.♖xd4 ♗xe5 26.♕e3 White has a technically won position.

25.dxe5

25...♖xd1+ An oversight in an inferior position. After 25...♗h3 both 26.♘d3 and 26.♕e3 give White good winning chances. At this point my opponent had roughly five minutes left, and only this can explain his next two bad moves.
26.♖xd1 ♕xe5 A continuation of the tactically bad idea 25...♖xd1+. The resistance would have been prolonged by 26...♗h3.
27.♖d8+

27...♔f7 By his own admission, Magnus overlooked that after 27...♔g7 28.♘e6+ ♗xe6 apart from 29.♕e7+ White also has 29.♕f8 mate.
28.♕f3+ ♗f5 29.♖xb8 ♕xb8

30.g4 White wins a piece.
30...♕b4 31.♘d3 Black resigned.

NOTES BY
Maxime Vachier-Lagrave

SI 4.8 – B96
Anish Giri
Maxime Vachier-Lagrave
Stavanger 2016 (2)

**1.e4 c5 2.♘f3 d6 3.d4 cxd4
4.♘xd4 ♘f6 5.♘c3 a6 6.♗g5**

Anish goes for it! A very unexpected but principled decision. For some reason I had had a look at my notes

> 'Anish goes for it! A very unexpected but principled decision.'

not long before the game, so I still had a few fresh memories of how to play this position.
6...e6 7.f4 h6 8.♗h4 ♕b6 9.a3

This is one of the issues of the move

order I went for to play the Poisoned Pawn, since the bishop can come back to f2 in case of ...♘c6. This makes the lines less forcing but still very sharp, and I generally don't mind that.
9...♗e7 10.♗f2 ♕c7 11.♕f3

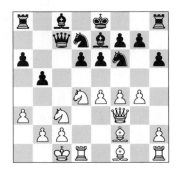

11...♘bd7
I had chosen 11...b5 against Sasha Grischuk at the London Chess Classic: 12.g4 ♘c6 (12...♗b7? is bad because of 13.g5 hxg5 14.fxg5 ♘fd7 15.g6) 13.♘xc6 (13.0-0-0 ♗b7 14.h4 d5!) 13...♕xc6, when 14.0-0-0 ♗b7 15.♗d3 would have been a bit dodgy, as my cherished ...d5 break is no longer possible: 15...d5 (15...g5 16.fxg5 hxg5 17.♗d4) 16.exd5 ♘xd5 17.♗e4, with a large advantage.
12.0-0-0 b5 13.g4

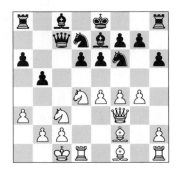

13...g5
The other option is 13...♗b7 14.♗g2 (14.h4 ♘c5 15.♗d3 d5 16.e5 ♘fe4 looks good for Black) 14...g5, but I prefer to keep the bishop on c8 for now to keep control of the e6-square in case of f5.
14.h4
Here 14.♗g2 ♖b8 15.♕h3!? b4! 16.axb4 ♖xb4 17.fxg5 ♘xg4! might become very double-edged, as

18.♕xg4 ♗xg5+ 19.♔b1 (19.♖d2 ♘e5 20.♕g3 ♘c4) 19...♕xc3 20.♘b3 ♕c7 looks good for Black.

14...gxf4 15.♗e2!

A great idea, already seen in correspondence chess. But I wasn't aware of that.

15...♖g8

After a while I decided in favour of this move, most importantly because it contains a subtle trap.

15...♘e5 16.♕xf4 ♘exg4 is the immediate option, but it leads to a very unpleasant position after the more or less forced sequence 17.♗xg4 e5 18.♘d5! (18.♕xf6? ♗xf6 19.♘d5 ♕d8 20.♘c6 ♗xg4 wouldn't be as smart as it looks) 18...♘xd5 19.♕f3 ♗xg4 (19...♘f4 20.♗xc8 ♖xc8 21.♖d2 followed by ♘f5 is worrisome) 20.♕xg4 ♘f6 21.♕f3 exd4 22.♗xd4 ♖g8 23.♗xf6 ♗xf6 24.♕xf6 ♖c8 25.♖h2 ♖g6 26.♕f4

ANALYSIS DIAGRAM

and White has a definite pull.

15...h5 16.g5 ♘g4 17.♕xf4! e5 18.♘d5 ♕b7 19.♕g3 is awful: 19...♘xf2 20.♕xf2 exd4 21.♘xe7 ♔xe7 22.♕xd4, and White is winning Objectively best is 15...♗b7. My

---

Maxime Vachier-Lagrave showed once again why he is seen as one of the greatest Najdorf experts in the world.

main concern was having to surrender the h-file, but apparently it's not the end of the world after 16.g5 ♘e5 17.♕xf4 ♘g6 18.♕f3 hxg5 19.hxg5 ♖xh1 20.♖xh1 ♘d7 21.♗e3 ♘de5 22.♕f2 0-0-0, and no sacrifice on b5 works quite yet. But things are still a bit dodgy, as there's no further plan available.

And finally there was 15...d5:

ANALYSIS DIAGRAM

A. 16.exd5 ♘e5! (16...♗b7 17.dxe6! ♗xf3 18.exd7+ would give White tremendous play for the queen and it never quite appealed to me), and now:
– 17.d6 scared me, but maybe with no good reason, as after 17...♘xf3 18.dxc7 ♘e5 19.♘dxb5 axb5 20.♗d4 ♘c6 21.♗xb5 ♗b7 Black should be fine.

– 17.♘cxb5? axb5 18.♘xb5 ♕b8 19.♕c3 ♘e4!! (19...♘xd5?? 20.♖xd5). I had completely missed this great defensive shot, which completely turns the tables: 20.♘c7+ ♔f8 21.♕xe5 ♗f6.

B. 16.g5! I didn't fully assess the strength of this move, since 16.exd5 was more of a concern to me: 16...♘e5 17.♕g2 ♘xe4 (17...♖g8 18.exd5 ♗b7 19.♕h3! ♘xd5 20.♘xe6, with a winning attack) 18.♘xe4 dxe4 19.♕xe4 ♗b7 20.♘xe6!

ANALYSIS DIAGRAM

20...fxe6 21.♗h5+ ♔f8 22.♕xf4+ ♔g8 23.♗f7+ ♔h7 24.g6+ ♔g7 25.♗d4 ♗f6 26.♖hf1 ♘d3+ 27.♖xd3 ♕xf4+ 28.♖xf4 e5 29.♖xf6 ♔xf6 30.♗c3, and Black ends up with an endgame that is very difficult to hold.

16.♖dg1?

Now my break attempt is much more powerful, as the white rook has left the d-file. But Anish wanted to keep his other rook on the h-file in case it was opened.

Instead, 16.g5! was the most principled move, and it seems to work:

– 16...♘e5 17.♕xf4 hxg5 (17...♘fg4 was the move that concerned Anish, but it fails to 18.♗xg4! hxg5 19.♕g3 gxh4 20.♖xh4 ♗xh4 21.♕xh4 ♘xg4 22.♖g1, and White wins material) 18.hxg5 ♘fd7 19.♘xe6!.

ANALYSIS DIAGRAM

The shot that I had underestimated, since otherwise (if my knights got to g6 and e5) things wouldn't be all that brutal. 19...fxe6 20.♖h7! ♗b7 21.♕h5+ ♔d8 22.g6, and I'm too cramped to defend: 22...♗f6 23.♗g4! ♘xg6 24.♖xd7+! ♕xd7 25.♕xf6+ ♔c7 26.♗c5! ♖af8 27.♕d4 ♖d8 28.♗b6+ ♔b8 29.♗xd8 ♖xd8 30.♕f6, with a technically winning position.

– 16...hxg5 17.hxg5 ♖xg5 18.♖h8+ ♖g8 19.♖xg8+ ♘xg8 20.e5 ♗b7 21.♘xe6 would win on the spot, and I didn't need to calculate lines to realize that.

Actually, 16.♕xf4! worked as well: 16...e5 17.♕xh6 exd4 (17...♘g6 18.♘e6! is crushing after 18...♗b7 19.♘g7+ ♔d8 20.♕h8+ ♗f8 21.g5) 18.♗xd4 ♗b7 19.♖hf1, and Black is in trouble again: 19...♘xg4 20.♗xg4 ♖xg4 21.♖xf7! ♔xf7 22.♕h5+ ♖g6 23.♕h7+ ♔e8 24.♕xg6+ ♔d8 25.♕g8+ ♘f8 26.♖f1, with a terrifying attack.

16...d5!

Now this break works much better.
17.exd5

I thought 17.g5 was the only way to complicate matters. I calculated the following: 17...♘e5 18.♕h3 ♘xe4 19.gxh6 ♖h8 20.♘xe4 dxe4 21.h7 ♖xh7 22.♖g8+ ♗f8, but I wasn't as certain as the computer that White has no real resources here.

17...♘e5

17...♗b7 would also work, but again allowing the queen sacrifice felt unnecessary: 18.dxe6 (18.♘c6 ♗f8!) 18...♗xf3 19.exd7+ ♕xd7 20.♗xf3 ♖c8 21.g5 ♖xc3! 22.bxc3 ♘d5 23.gxh6 ♖h8, although Black still has the upper hand.

18.♕h3 exd5

19.♖e1

After 19.♘f5 ♗xf5 20.gxf5 ♖xg1+ 21.♖xg1 Black has 21...0-0-0! 22.♔b1 ♗c5, with a clear advantage.

Alternatively, 19.♗f3! isn't too natural, but might have been a good resource, forcing me once again to find 19...♔f8! (19...♕d6! could also be good to just pick up pawn g4, although it doesn't look good at first sight...) 20.♔b1 h5 21.♘xd5 ♘xd5 22.♗xd5 ♗xg4 23.♕h2 ♖d8 with a clear advantage after the forced line 24.♕xf4 ♖xd5 25.♖xg4 ♖xg4 26.♘e6+ ♔g8 27.♘xc7 ♖xf4 28.♘xd5 ♖xf2 29.♘xe7+ ♔g7, although White might be able to hold this.

19...♔f8!?

Unnecessary, according to the computer, but preventing any sacrifice on b5 looked good to me, as the ♖e1 now looks stupid.

The computer prefers 19...h5, since 20.♗xb5+ axb5 21.♘dxb5 ♕b8 22.♗d4 ♘exg4 won't yield White anything.

20.♘f5

On 20.♕g2 ♗xg4 21.♘xd5 ♕b7! would win a piece after 22.♘xf4 ♕xg2 23.♘xg2 ♗xe2 24.♖xe2 ♖xg2 25.♖xe5 ♖xf2.

20...♗xf5 21.gxf5 ♗c5!

Obtaining complete control of the dark squares. If White could consolidate his king now, things wouldn't be so terrible yet, but here he's just too late to prevent himself from being wiped away. It was actually quite unexpected how fast things got really bad for White, but all my pieces were suddenly in the right place.

22.♕f1

22.♗xc5+ ♕xc5, followed by either ...d4 or ...♖g3, would be the start of a mating attack.

22...d4 23.♘b1

23.♘d1 ♖c8 24.♗d3 ♘fg4 25.♔b1 ♘e3 would be really bad as well.

23...♘e4 24.♗f3 ♘xf2!

Winning on the spot, in more than one way.

25.♗xa8

25...♘ed3+ 25...d3 26.♘c3 d2+ 27.♔xd2 ♗e3+ was also more than enough, but I preferred the text, since it was completely forcing and because I liked the final position.

26.♔d2

Or 26.cxd3 ♗xa3+ 27.♔d2 ♗b4+ 28.♔e2 f3+! 29.♔xf3 (29.♗xf3 ♕c2+) 29...♕g3+ 30.♔e2 ♕e3 mate.

26...♘xe1 27.♕xf2

27...d3! 28.♕xe1 ♗e3+

And White resigned in view of 29.♔xd3 ♕c4 mate.

NOTES BY
Pentala Harikrishna

FR 4.4 – C11
Anish Giri
Pentala Harikrishna
Stavanger 2016 (6)

Prior to the Norway event, Anish had participated in the Candidates' tournament and drawn all of his 14 games. This led to numerous jokes circulating online! However, the battles between me and Anish have been mostly decisive! We both were on 50 per cent at this point and I had won a nice game against Li Chao in the previous round and was ready for a fight.

1.e4 Anish has a very broad repertoire, which makes it very hard to predict his opening choice. Probably he chose what he did based on the fact that I had played the French against Nils Grandelius.

1...e6 2.d4 d5 3.♘c3 ♘f6

4.e5 My game against Nils continued 4.♗g5 dxe4 5.♘xe4 ♗e7 6.♗xf6 gxf6. My results with the Burn Variation have been good. I had an advantage in the middlegame, which I later misplayed, giving him some chances. Later he missed his chances too and we drew after an eventful game!

4...♘fd7 5.f4 c5 6.♘f3 ♗e7!?

This move has its pros and cons. Black is basically trying to delay ...♘c6 and retain the option of playing ...♗a6, as in the game. On the other hand, Black loses flexibility and has committed himself to playing the ♗e7 variation.

The alternative is 6...♘c6 7.♗e3, and now:

ANALYSIS DIAGRAM

7...cxd4 8.♘xd4 ♕b6. Simen Agdestein defended this complicated variation successfully in the 2014 edition of Norway Chess.
After 7...♕b6 8.♘a4 ♕a5+ 9.c3 White is doing very well.
After 7...a6 8.♕d2 ♗e7 9.dxc5 ♘xc5 10.0-0-0 0-0

ANALYSIS DIAGRAM

the main position in the ♗e7 variation arises. By delaying ...♘c6 Black's idea in the game is to retain the option of developing it to d7 depending upon White's choice of moves.

7.♗e3 0-0 8.♕d2 b6

This is the main point of delaying ...♘c6, since White can no longer play dxc5 and 0-0-0 would be met by ...c4 later in the game.

9.♘d1

This is the most challenging move. Me and my second Ragger briefly looked at it and found some interesting ideas here.

9.h4!? is quite an interesting possibility which requires further practical tests.

9.♗e2 ♘c6 will transpose to one of the main lines: 10.0-0 ♗b7. Tons of theory here!

9...a5

There is no point in playing ...♗a6 before White develops, since this would save White a tempo, so it is better to expand on the queenside.

10.c3

After 10.a4 I wanted to play 10...♘c6 (as 10...♗a6 would be met by 11.♗b5) 11.c3 ♗b7 (after 11...♗a6 12.♗xa6 ♖xa6 13.0-0 White is better, since Black has to waste some tempi to push ...b5) 12.♗e2 ♕c8 13.0-0 ♗a6, with unclear play.

10...a4 11.♗d3 ♗a6

12.0-0

At first sight 12.f5 appears very dangerous. However, Black is well developed and White's attack won't succeed: 12...exf5 13.♗xf5 (13.0-0 ♖e8 favours Black. This motif of vacating the f8-square for the knight is always useful in such positions) 13...♘c6 14.h4 a3 15.bxa3 ♖e8 16.e6 ♘f8 17.exf7+ ♔xf7, with a good position for Black.

12...♘c6

13.♗xa6 Since I consider 13.f5 in all scenarios, I did so here, too! I intended to take on f5 with the pawn, and the following variation shows that Black is doing fine here: 13...exf5 14.♗xa6 ♖xa6 15.♕d3 b5!. This is

a nice move, as White is not planning to take on b5 and Black is creating a square for the knight on d7. At the same time, the rook on a6 is doing a good job by taking care of the sixth rank, while if need be it can swing over to kingside!: 16.♕xf5 cxd4 17.cxd4 ♘b6, with firm control of the light squares.

13...♖xa6

14.f5

This move is very tempting, but after Black plays 14...b5, White has to decide on what he really wants to do (whether to resolve the central tension with fxe6 or sacrifice a pawn with f5-f6 or maintain the tension!) So in my opinion it is better to play 14.♕d3 first.

Mihail Marin:
Winning against the Classical Slav

This DVD offers White a complete repertoire against the classical Slav, a popular opening, in which Black can choose from a wide range of plans. In the Slav White often has more space but to turn this into an advantage he needs to know the typical strategic and tactical motifs of the opening and has to develop a feeling for the nuances of the position. The videos on this DVD give White a repertoire with concrete variations against all main lines Black can play and also show the typical strategic and tactical ideas of the Slav and the hidden subtleties of the position. This makes it easier to memorize the main variations and makes sure that White knows what to do when the current theory develops. Most of the videos are interactive, offering tactical exercises in typical positions to help the reader to understand and remember the material better. In addition to the videos the DVD also offers a number of databases. One database contains the analysis presented in the videos, another database has extensively annotated illustrative games. As additional material the DVD comes with two articles by the author about the Slav that were published earlier in the ChessBase Magazine. Video running time: 6 hours 10 min.

29,90 €

Sam Collins:
Queen's Gambit Declined - A repertoire for Black based on the Lasker Variation

On this DVD, Sam Collins presents a repertoire for Black based on the rock-solid Lasker variation, reinvigorated with new ideas by former World Champion Vishy Anand and forming the cornerstone of many strong GM repertoires today. With the exception of the Catalan, all the significant variations after 1.d4 d5 2.c4 e6 are covered, including White's deviations with Bxf6 and Bf4, and the critical Exchange Variation. Recent attempts by White to launch a kingside pawn storm with g4 and h4 have also been covered in detail. No other opening can boast a better pedigree than the QGD, having been contested by World Champions with both colours. In going through the material, in addition to learning an opening against 1.d4 which can be played for life, the viewer will also become closely acquainted with a large number of the most important grandmaster games of recent years. Video running time: 5 hours 50 min. With interactive training videos and an exclusive training database with more than 200 model games.

29,90 €

Sergei Tiviakov:
Learning from the World Champions

From amateurs to professionals – players of all levels know how difficult it is to learn chess strategy and how much time and effort it takes to improve middlegame play. The author of this DVD has a solution - suggesting and demonstrating what he believes to be the easiest and most affordable method - learning from the World Champions! With famous classical examples from the works of the giants, the author talks in detail about principles of chess and methods of play that we can use during every stage of the game. Each example of World Champion play is followed by a similar example from the practice of the author, proving that his method works! A great deal of incredibly useful aspects are discussed and lot of tips offered on how to improve your play in 25 examples with 5 hours of video.

29,90 €

CHESSBASE GMBH · OSTERBEKSTRASSE 90A · D-22083 HAMBURG · TEL ++(49) 40/639060-12 · FAX ++(49) 40/6301282 · WWW.CHESSBASE.COM · INFO@CHESSBASE.COM

CHESSBASE DEALER: NEW IN CHESS · P.O. Box 1093 · NL-1810 KB Alkmaar · phone (+31)72 5127137 · fax (+31)72 5158234 · WWW.NEWINCHESS.COM

The point of 14.♕d3! is that it prevents Black from achieving ...b5 easily: 14...c4 15.♕c2 f5 16.exf6 ♘xf6. White's position seems slightly better, as Black does not have a clear plan to improve his position.

ANALYSIS DIAGRAM

However, I intended to continue with ...♕c8, ...b5, ...♗d6 and ...♘d8. It is not entirely clear to me what kind of progress White would make here.

14...b5

14...exf5 15.♕d3 b5 16.♕xf5 cxd4 17.cxd4 ♘b6 would transpose to one of the variations I gave above. I thought 14...b5 would give Black more chances.

15.fxe6

15.f6 is the most challenging move here. I calculated several variations, as I expected Anish to go for this. But Black is doing fine in this variation as well: 15...gxf6 16.exf6 (16.♗h6 leads nowhere, since Black will happily sacrifice the exchange, because he has an excellent centre and a nice structure: 16...fxe5 17.♗xe5 ♘cxe5 18.dxe5 ♘xe5) 16...♘xf6 17.♗h6 ♘e4 18.♕e1 f5!.

15...fxe6 16.♕e2 ♕b6

17.♘f2 Whether right or wrong, White had to play 17.a3, I felt. White cannot afford to allow Black's pawns on a3 and b4.

17...a3 18.b3

The engine suggests 18.b4. Obviously, I did not calculate this move over the board. I am giving the readers a funny computer line to sit back and enjoy ☺: 18...cxb4 19.cxb4 ♖a4 20.♘h3 ♖xb4 21.♘fg5 ♘d8 22.♕h5 h6 23.♘f3 ♖f7

ANALYSIS DIAGRAM

everything here is 0.00!!! to the engine. I wouldn't be surprised if this is lost for Black.

18...b4!

White's position is quite difficult here already.

19.dxc5 ♗xc5 20.♗xc5 ♘xc5 21.c4 ♘e4 22.cxd5 exd5

23.e6 I think Anish had probably missed 23.♔h1 ♘xf2+ 24.♖xf2 ♘xe5 when he went for this variation. If White can get in ♔h1, then the white position is completely fine. However, the ♘xe5 tactic makes it impossible for White to move the king.

23...♘e7

Apparently, 3200+ thinks 23...♖aa8 is the best. One cannot argue with it.

24.♔h1 ♘c3 25.♕d3 h6 26.♘d1

This is the final mistake. White is losing a pawn and Black's knight on c3 is a monster, and the rest of the game does not need any commentary.

26...♕b5 27.♕xb5 ♘xb5 28.♘f2 ♖xe6 29.♘d3 ♘c6 30.♖fc1 ♘c3 31.♘xb4 ♘xb4 32.♖xc3 ♖e2 33.♖c7 ♖a8 34.♘d4 ♖xa2 35.♖f1 ♖d2 36.h3 a2

White resigned.

Norway was a nice experience for me and I had an opportunity to take part in some interesting games. After the first rest-day activities both my play and results improved! I would like to thank all the people who helped me prepare for Norway. ∎

Magnus Carlsen:

'I feel that I am closer to the start than to the end of my prime'

At long last, Magnus Carlsen won the finest tournament on his native soil and he is happy, no question, but looking back on Altibox Norway Chess in an interview with **DIRK JAN TEN GEUZENDAM,** the World Champion seems to be more interested in griping and grousing over the flaws in his play and in brooding on how he can improve himself. 'My approach and the games that I played were just complacency-riddled.'

We meet half an hour before the closing dinner. As the guests are flowing into the lobby of the Scandic Stavanger City Hotel and waiters are making their rounds with welcome drinks, we retreat to a quiet corridor. Magnus Carlsen is dressed in 'elegant casual' style, as the tournament rules stipulate: a suit with the names of his main sponsors, no tie, and, as people do these days – but not required by the tournament rules – carrying a small bottle of water. By now, 24 hours

after his last game, he has had more than enough time to think about what the win in Norway Chess means to him, if only because every journalist he has spoken to so far has asked him this question.

Most people that he will talk to during dinner are sure to ask him again, and I would have loved to come up with something more original, but before I know it I have asked him how badly he wanted this one. And not showing any surprise, he calmly replies: 'I really wanted to win, of course, but I was treating it like a normal tournament. I always felt that it would be special to win,

but that's not how it felt during the tournament.'

I tell him that on my arrival in Stavanger I had had a talk with Jøran Aulin-Jansson, the tournament director, who opined that if Magnus started with 2½ from 3, he would win. That didn't sound like a brave prediction, but I knew what he meant. He was not only referring to Magnus's programme in the first three rounds (White against Harikrishna and Grandelius, Black against Topalov), but also to his hesitant start in so many tournaments. This time he needed a quick start for a change.

A happy Magnus Carlsen at the press conference after he has beaten Pavel Eljanov and finally added Norway Chess to his collection. 'I always felt that it would be special to win, but that's not how it felt during the tournament.'

'Yeah. Sure. Obviously, winning the blitz tournament was important, so I got to pick a number that was very favourable for me, that certainly helped. The last game (against Giri) was not great, obviously, but in general I played better than expected.'

Did you do anything different before the tournament compared to the past years?
'I had a training camp, which certainly helped. I felt I was in pretty poor chess shape before that. I wasn't seeing things very well in training games, in analysis, but afterwards it was sort of alright.'

Following his flashy 2½/3 start, the key game against Vladimir Kramnik in Round 7 gave Carlsen a confidence-inspiring one-point lead with only two rounds to go. Before the tournament he had said that if there was one player he wanted to beat, it was Kramnik. In a jocular reaction at the initial press-conference the Russian had retorted that he wanted to beat everyone. Carlsen did beat Kramnik in a brutal and one-sided game. He had such an advantage out of the opening that he went to the confession box during the game to thank his second Jon-Ludvig Hammer on Norwegian television.

'Yes, that was Hammer's idea. I didn't talk about it with Hammer, but apparently he had spoken with Peter (Heine Nielsen). Peter had told me some days before that Hammer had found something against this line. So I was kind of hoping for this to happen, but obviously I had expected Vlady to play something else. I was definitely pleasantly surprised when he went for this.'

Kramnik remains one of the big guys and he is always a contender for first place, wherever he goes. Did it give you particular pleasure that you beat him that way?
'No, the game was over so quickly. It doesn't give the same satisfaction to beat someone who doesn't play at his full strength. We all know he had an off-day. I was happy to get the win obviously, but the game in itself was nothing special.'

Still, by that time you must have felt that things were going really well.
'Yeah, but I think I became complacent, actually. My approach and the games that I played were just complacency-riddled. In general, the energy level wasn't very high and I didn't make any brave decisions, just trying to take the path of least resistance, all the way. I was scoring well, so although I realized that my state of mind wasn't really right, I didn't care too much.'

You made an energetic impression. You maybe even looked unusually lively during the tournament.
'Yes (laughs), it was just that my play wasn't showing that.'

You didn't win the game against Giri, which was obviously another one you wanted to win. Is that frustrating?
'No, it's a normal result. But I was upset by the way I played, especially because he played very superficially for a while and actually gave me chances to exploit. I mean, he handled the first part of the middlegame better than I did; he was

slightly better but it was probably very drawish. Then he played very poorly for 10 moves and gave me chances. I was upset that I didn't take them.'

You made another draw against Anish, who got a lot of flak for his draws, particularly on the Internet, even when he does fight, as in the Candidates'. What is your take on that?
'I think he generally plays well, but at the critical junctures he maybe lacks the confidence or courage to make the choices he has to make. I don't know. In this tournament, I think we'll all agree, he just played poorly. That didn't have anything to do with draws.'

Criticism on the web can be harsh and simplistic. Is it something that has an effect on you? That you read things and think, what kind of crap is this?
'No, not really. I mean, I think I know myself and the other players better than the people who write such things. It can be entertaining, but it's not something you listen to too much. And certainly not something that you get offended by (laughs).'

Back to the tournament. Everything seemed to go smoothly and then, in the last round but one, you lose to Aronian. This is always a possibility, of course, but still it came as a surprise. I thought you were in control and that something like this was not going to happen.
'It was not a good day for me. I was not very energetic that particular day, but most of all it's about complacency again. I didn't want to make any hard

choices, basically, and then I was outplayed very quickly. I couldn't even pull myself together to fight back, even though I had very decent fighting chances. Especially, as he'll admit himself, since he has a history of not converting advantages against me. But the sheer number of things I missed during that game is just incredible. I realized at that point that something had to change.'

Last year, before St. Louis, Levon and you spent time together in the Hamptons, training a bit. You are on good terms. This sounds great, but at the same time you might think that it sometimes complicates matters.
'No. It might hurt a little less to lose, but apart from that, no. I feel I have always been on decent terms with Levon, but every time I lose to him, which fortunately hasn't happened too often in the last six or seven years, is just as annoying as against anyone else.'

Now, suddenly, your tournament had been turned upside down and you found yourself in a must-win situation in the final round. Did you feel you had the strength to get yourself ready for the last game? Were there any doubts?
'I wasn't so sure, but I was of course encouraged by the fact that I have a very good record against Pavel (Eljanov). And obviously, after his unexpected losses in his last two games, he was not going to be in a great state psychologically. As it happened, I didn't make a great opening choice and the position was nothing special,

but then he started to make some poor choices and it all went quite smoothly actually.'

The day before you lost to Levon, you had taken your undefeated record from 41 to 42. It was a bit amusing for you to keep that record so briefly and even made me think of Sergey Bubka, who always improved his records by the minimum...
'I think that one thing is that lots and lots of people have had longer streaks than that, so I don't think I should be focusing on that. But on the other hand, it was also making me complacent, yeah. That I hadn't lost a game in such a long time, the confidence that I could save all bad positions. And also that I was thinking, let's not risk it, as long as I don't lose, it's fine. I think it's good to have that out of the world. That's probably something I needed.'

You finally won Norway Chess. Do you have a better understanding now of what went wrong in the previous ones?
'Again, this is the best Norway Chess tournament I have played and again I am not very happy with the way I played. I think I came close twice, and last year was something that happens once every 10 years or so.'

It was probably the question no one dared to ask last year, but did you in fact feel after that first-round loss (on time against Topalov because Carlsen didn't know the time-control) that the tournament was out of the window?
'No, not at all. But it probably contrib-

BEACH & CHESS
EUROPE 2016 Summer Guide
www.travelforchess.com

Talking to the press after his unexpected loss to Levon Aronian in the last-round-but-one. 'The sheer number of things I missed during that game is just incredible.'

uted to me sort of not fighting in the way I should have in my next game against Caruana. When I got a bad position, I went down pretty easily. Then I still kind of believed in it, but when I didn't win a completely winning position against Anish it was pretty much over.'

This is your fourth tournament victory in a row. Many people are saying: He is back to his best chess. Do you share that feeling?
'No, not really. I can do much better and I need to be sharper. I realize that the level I am playing at right now is usually good enough to fight for first place, but for me it's not enough. I know I can do better and so I should be better.'

The general feeling here was that you were very relaxed. Many evenings you were down in the bar playing Avalon, whereas you often barely mingle with the other players or you don't go to the restaurant or the hotel bar. Was that a change of approach?
'It also depends on the other people that are there. Whether they are people I like to hang out with. It's easier here in Norway to actually be more social. My feeling is that it can be positive, not that it's always negative. I mean, if I am feeling good I usually play well.'

I don't know the rules of Avalon, but as far as I can make out, it's a game in which it helps if you're good at deceiving people. Is that something you find amusing?
'No, I think I am a terrible liar, but I think most people are too, so there is nothing special there. I think most people believe they are better at lying than they really are (laughs).'

You usually come across as frank and open in interviews and the way you present yourself, but there are times when people might wonder if you're playing a part.
'Yeah. I don't know. What I can say is that most of the time what I say is what I feel and people can choose to believe that or not (laughs).'

Six months from now you will play the World Championship match. What place does it occupy in your head?
'Well, during the tournament it isn't there at all. I have played World Championship matches before and I don't see why thinking about it now would help me. Here I was focused on this tournament. Of course, between tournaments I do think about it once in a while. It can be pleasant, but it's also a headache. I think that's the way it always is. Like, before this tournament I was excited to play, but I also

had doubts about my form, about my preparation. These thoughts are always there and they are much the same thoughts as before a world championship match. You're never completely sure of yourself. It's always a fight with your own mind.'

And that's purely a one-on-one with yourself. Because people will say, you just won four tournaments in a row...
'Yeah. Of course, of course. I mean, I am my own harshest critic and most of it is in my mind, most of it is not known to people outside...'

Do you express these thoughts to your seconds?
'Sometimes.'

What phase of your career do you feel you are in?
'I don't know. I feel that I have been in the game for a long time already and I think if you do the right things, you can be good for a very long time. I feel that I am closer to the start than to the end of my prime. I enjoy playing and I still have so much to work on. It's very obvious to me that I can still be much better, and from tournament to tournament I am trying to learn something new about chess or about myself. But it's not easy. I've got to be better now. I had a few poor tournaments last year. Then I felt like I turned myself around, but now I need to take the next steps. I cannot remain stuck at the level I am at now... not only as regards chess, but as regards the combination of chess and psychology.'

Because you are the favourite in the match, but you'll meet an opponent that will be armed to the teeth.
'It's not about that. It's about me wanting to perform at my best, not about just something that may or may not be good enough.' ∎

Pawn Power

She may be more famous for her piece play, but **JUDIT POLGAR** certainly appreciates a good pawn when she sees one.

Even though I was aware of the magic behind the pawn's ability to become a queen, I did not pay too much attention to my pawns as a kid. I would recklessly neglect the 'health' and integrity of my structure for the sake of piece activity, and more than once I suffered the bitter consequences of prematurely throwing my pawns ahead. 'Pawns never move backwards' is a basic principle I only started taking seriously much later.

But when pawn play took concrete contours, as in the case of a promotion race, I was quite accurate. Here is an example from my best year as a teenager:

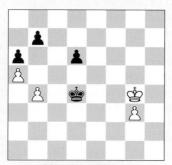

Sigfusson-Polgar
Reykjavik 1988
position after 52.♔g4

Black's turn to move offers me an extra tempo in the race, but if White could approach with his king, things would turn into a 'remote white passed pawn' pattern.
52...♔e4! Blocking the enemy king's access to the d-file.
53.♔h3 ♔f3
I invested a tempo in preventing the white king's approach but foresaw that I would get it back with interest in the following forced sequence.
54.g4 ♔f4 55.♔h4 d5 56.g5 ♔f5!
Forcing the white king to occupy a vulnerable square. **57.♔h5 d4 58.g6 d3 59.g7 d2 60.g8♕ d1♕+**

Promoting with check retrieves the tempo, forcing a transposition back to a pawn ending. **61.♔h6 ♕h1+ 62.♔g7 ♕g2+ 63.♔f8 ♕xg8+ 64.♔xg8 ♔e6 65.♔f8 ♔d5 66.♔e7 ♔c4** 0-1.

Pawn races can take on a much more subtle and at the same time more violent shape in the middlegame.

Serper-Nikolaidis
St Petersburg 1993
position after 29...♕e8

White has sacrificed two pieces for the attack, but his resources seem almost exhausted. His advanced pawns offer him some hope, but he should not neglect the force of the f2-pawn. For instance: 30.♕xe8+? ♔xe8 31.♖e7+ ♔f8! 32.c6 ♘g3+!! 33.hxg3 (or if 33.♔xf2 ♘f5 the knight joins the fight with decisive effect) 33...hxg3, with inevitable promotion of the f-pawn. This is the first moment when we feel there is a true pawn race going on. But White found a spectacular way to speed up the advance of his pawns:
30.♖f7+!! ♕xf7 31.♕c8+ ♕e8

32.d7! A recurrent theme, as we will see. **32...♔f7 33.dxe8♕+ ♖xe8 34.♕b7+ ♔e7** White has won a rook for a pawn, but is still left with a slight material disadvantage, so he needs to act decisively. **35.c6!**

The second pawn advances in similar circumstances as its colleague.
35...e4! The best chance. Black clears the e5-square, threatening 36...♖xb7 37.cxb7

♗e5 and setting up a different pawn race at the same time.

36.c7 e3 It looks as if Black has won the race, but White has a simple way to dismantle Black's mechanism.

37.♕d5+ ♔f6 37...♔e6 38.♕xe6+ is similar to the game. **38.♕d6+ ♔f7 39.♕d5+** Move repetition aimed at reaching the time-control before taking a committal decision. **39...♔f6 40.♕d6+ ♔f7**

41.♕xe7+ ♔xe7 42.c8♕ After winning the second rook for a pawn White also quickly won the game. **42...♗h6 43.♕c5+ ♔e8 44.♕b5+ ♔d8 45.♕b6+ ♔d7 46.♕xg6 e2+ 47.♔xf2 ♗e3+ 48.♔e1** 1-0.

On the way to developing my technical skills I started treasuring pawns and structure more. In the next game I gladly sacrificed my pieces in order to get a compact and mobile pawn mass in the centre, exactly the opposite of what I used to do as a kid.

Karpov-Polgar
Buenos Aires 2000
position after 16.♖ad1

16...♘d5 Hardly a surprise for Karpov, who had faced this position twice before.

Each time he answered 17.♗xe4 without achieving anything. My last move was not a real sacrifice, as after 17.cxd5? cxd5 White has no adequate way to get out of the pin. If 18.♕b2 then 18...b4 traps the bishop anyway.

17.♗b2!? Even though I had not expected this, I knew I would not like to withdraw my knight, so I replied relatively quickly: **17...f5! 18.cxd5 cxd5 19.♕b1 b4**

Black has only two pawns for her knight, but my centre strongly restricts the white minor pieces. In order to put my pawns into motion I needed to undermine White's only central pawn on d4.

20.♘f1 ♕b6 21.f3 ♗f6 22.♘e3

White seems to have consolidated and even got some activity, but my next move, planned in advance, shatters his position.

22...♖c3! For the sake of putting my pawns into motion I did not mind playing a whole rook down!

23.♗xc3 bxc3 Black has full compensation, but the game has become very complex. The next phase is marred by mutual inaccuracies but is illustrative for my idea to sacrifice the knight and the exchange. For a full analysis of the game you may wish to check my comments in

Judit Polgar Teaches Chess – From GM to Top Ten.

24.♘c2? 24.fxe4 fxe4 25.♘c2! is safer, although White does not have an advantage.

24...e5?! 24...♗xd4+!. **25.♘e3 exd4 26.♘xd5 ♕c5 27.♘xf6+ ♖xf6**

A picturesque position! White has a rook for only two pawns, but is in danger of being crushed by the central phalanx.

28.b4! Getting some elbow room for the queen and embarking on the only way to save the game.

If 28.fxe4? then 28...d3+ 29.♔h1 c2 retrieves the rook, preserving the advantage based on the advanced d3-pawn.

28...♖c4 29.♕b3 d3 30.♕xc4+ ♗xc4 31.♗f1 ♖c6 32.fxe4 d2 33.b5 ♖c5 34.♗xc4+ ♖xc4

35.exf5 If 35.♖f1 ♖xe4 36.♔f2 (not 36.a4? ♖e2, followed by ...c2, with complete white paralysis) 36...♔f7, White would sooner or later have to liquidate with ♖xd2 in order to avoid the worst.

35...dxe1♕+ 36.♖xe1 ♔f7 37.♖c1 ♔f6 38.♔f2 ♖a4 39.♖c2 ♔xf5 40.♔e3 ♖a5 ½-½.

Despite the peaceful result, this was quite a memorable game to have played against a World Champion! ∎

Tucking away your bishop

Even in the most hideous of places your bishop may be of use, as **ARTHUR VAN DE OUDEWEETERING** shows.

Porreca-Bronstein
Belgrade 1954
position after 11.♖e1

11...♗g8! An exclamation mark from Bronstein. His logic was that he needed to protect f7 to castle queenside and to prevent sacrifices on e6 in order to castle kingside (after the necessary ...e7-e6). Afterwards the bishop would be able to return to h7. Despite the fact that White had committed himself to h2-h4 and castled kingside later, should such a slow plan not lead to disaster? Objectively, 11...♘b6 12.♗b3 0-0-0 13.♗xf7 e5 14.♘e6 ♕xf7 15.♘xd8 ♔xd8 16.dxe5+ ♘fd5 seems best: materially White is OK, but Black has the more smoothly developing pieces. **12.♘d3 e6 13.♗f4 ♗d6 14.♗xd6 ♕xd6 15.♘f5 ♕f8** Another nine points are hidden in a passive position. **16.♕f3?!** 16.♘f4 0-0-0 17.♗xe6 seems to be the best try and was indicated by Bronstein himself. Play may continue 17...fxe6 18.♘g6 exf5 19.♘xf8 ♖xf8 20.♕d2 ♗d5 21.b3, with an active queen, while the black pieces have a hard time to find strongholds and coordination. **16...0-0-0 17.♘g3** Now, miraculously, Black's plan seems to have worked: on the next move, his bishop will return to

h7. After the concrete alternative 17.♗a6 ♘b8 (17...♘d5 18.c4) 18.♗xb7+ ♔xb7 19.♘c5+ ♔a8 20.♕b3 (20.b4 exf5 21.b5 was a suggestion of Bronstein's, but it can be refuted by the prosaic 21...♖xd4 22.b6 ♕xc5) 20...♖d7 White's attack is stopped in its tracks.

17...♗h7 18.a4 ♗xd3 19.♗xd3 ♕d6 The Italian has clearly played too passively, and now Black's general ideas have been accomplished. Bronstein himself acknowledged the artificial aspect of his manoeuvre, but added these true words: if you fear sporting and creative failures in chess, you will never manage to come up with anything new.

Yet Bronstein's idea was not entirely new:

Treybal-Nimzowitsch
Semmering 1926
position after 12.♘h5

You will have guessed that Nimzowitsch now produced:

12...♗g8!? Of course, Nimzowitsch introduced the concept of the 'mysterious rook move' – to which I devoted a chapter in *Train Your Chess Pattern Recognition* – but this bishop move is not so mysterious. Rather than serving a prophylactic

purpose, it looks like a desperate defence, as some simple variations show: 12...♘bd7 13.♘xf7 ♔xf7 14.♕xe6+; 12...♘xh5 13.♕xh5 g6 14.♕f3 ♕c7 15.♗f6 ♖g8 16.♗xe6. In the game Nimzowitsch got away with it – he scraped a draw (and at some point he was even given the chance to play for more – see move 15).

13.f4 13.♗f4 ♘bd7 14.0-0-0 ♘xh5 15.♕xh5 ♘f6 16.♕f3 seems simple and strong. **13...♘bd7 14.f5 ♘xe5 15.♕xe5?** 15.♘xf6+ gxf6 16.dxe5, with an excellent position. **15...♕b8** 15...♘xh5 16.fxe6 f5!. **16.♘xf6+ gxf6 17.♕xb8+ ♖xb8** with a clear White advantage, which gradually disappeared (½-½, 38).

So did we solve the riddle: the stronger player is always right? Not quite: here is an example in which the passive over-protection (Nimzowitsch!) of e6 seems very appropriate.

Titov-Yudasin
Kostroma 1985
position after 19.♘g2

19...♗g8! Even if Yudasin knew the first two examples – which obviously would have made his decision easier – I still think it is quite an achievement to come up with the text-move. If 19...♗g6 20.♘xg5 (20.♗xg5 ♖xh3) 20...♘xe5 (20...♗xg5 21.♗xg5 ♖xh3 22.♗h4 ♘xe5? 23.♕e2) 21.♗f4 ♗d6 22.♕e2, and now, after 22... f6, e6 is not protected: 23.♘xe6.

20.♗xg5 20.♘xg5 ♘xe5 21.♗f4 ♗d6 22.♕e2 f6. **20...♗xg5 21.♘xg5 ♘xe5 22.♘f4** Again, 22.♕e2 can be met by 22...f6. **22...♕d6 23.c4 f6 24.♘f3 ♘g6! 25.♕d2 ♘xf4 26.♕xf4 ♕xf4 27.gxf4 ♖xh3** And the World Championship Candidate converted his advantage.

In 2005, I visited St. Petersburg with two Dutch chess friends for a couple of training lessons at Khalifman's chess school. In one of these, Alexander Shashin, in the short time he had, failed to convince us of his own special method, which was later to be disclosed in the English language in his book *Best Play*. He did impress us, though, with the following game, especially with White's 17th move.

Capablanca-Molina/Ruiz
Buenos Aires consultation 1914
position after 16...♗f7

17.c4!! Between the many algorithms in Shashin's book you can find the following sensible words: 'Black is suffocating: he suffers from a serious lack of suitable squares for his shiftless pieces. This is why it is good for Capablanca to refuse to trade bishops.' After 17.♗xf7 ♘xf7 suddenly the black knights are cooperating harmoniously. Now 18.g4 d5 19.g5 ♘d6 20.gxf6? gxf6 21.♗h6 ♖f7 suits Black perfectly.
17...c5?! Capablanca indicates 17...b5 as better. But the two black players apparently still thought it wise to lock in the a2-bishop even more.
18.g4 ♘g8 19.♗d2 b5 Repentance, but too late. If Black continues 'normally', White can slowly build up an attack thanks to his space advantage in this closed position, for example: 19...♘c6

'If you fear sporting and creative failures in chess, you will never manage to come up with anything new.'

20.♖f2 ♘d4 21.♘xd4 exd4 22.g5 fxg5 23.♗xg5 ♗h5 24.♖af1 ♘f6 25.♖g2, and White will repatriate his bishop starting with ♗b3.
20.g5 fxg5 21.♘xg5 ♘f6 22.♖f3 bxc4 22...♗h5 23.♖g3 h6 24.cxb5 hxg5 25.♗xg5, and ♖h3 is coming next. White is winning.

23.♘xh7! ♘xh7 24.♖h3 ♗g8 25.♗xc4 ♖f7 25...♘f7 26.f6 g6 27.♔h1, followed by ♖g1, with a winning attack.
26.♔h1!

Despite his extra piece, Black is remarkable helpless. Capa won smoothly after **26...b5 27.♗d5 ♖aa7 28.♖g1 ♖f6 29.♗g5 ♖af7 30.b3!** (1-0, 39)

Despite the clear justification, it still pains me to look at the a2-bishop even today. But there is a nice soothing com-

parison: Kramnik once stated that Black's bad light-squared Stonewall bishop is no worse than White's fianchettoed bishop on g2; the latter only appears more active, just like Black's bishop on f7 here.
Nor was this just an isolated incident from the past. Contemporary chess features similar ways to avoid exchanges. Here is another bishop buried alive.

Zhigalko-Mamedov
Denizli 2013
position after 13...♗e6

14.b3!? A novelty that has never been repeated since. White invariably opted for 14.♗xe6 fxe6 15.e5, which is of course a much firmer continuation. Contrary to the text-move, this will not expose you to possible ridicule from your colleagues. Zhigalko is brave enough to try and make something of his slight space advantage.
14...♘cd7 15.♘e2 15.♗b1!? was worth considering. It would have to be played sooner or later anyway.
15...d5 16.♘f4 ♖e8 17.♘xe6 fxe6 18.e5 ♗c5 19.♕g4 ♗xe3 20.♖xe3 ♕e7 21.c3 The bishop comes back into play – with the help of the e5-pawn White is developing an initiative on the kingside.
21...c5 22.♗b1 Understandable, but White could have postponed the 'burial' of the bishop a bit longer with 22.c4!, fixing the queenside in favourable fashion: 22...dxc4 (22...d4 23.♖ee1) 23.bxc4 ♘xa4 24.♗b1, with a dangerous initiative for the pawn. After **22...♘f8 23.h4 c4!** the game eventually ended in a draw.

Perhaps you will be able to consider similar ugly bishop moves now. When you actually execute them, make sure you have enough time for such a long-term strategy, especially in a closed position. ■

A notable lacuna in the vast accretion of chess literature is learned discourse on the topic of sex. Does carnal cavorting during a tournament help or hinder one's play? This vital subject – how to conduct oneself away from the board, with a view to maximising one's chess results – ought to be of great importance for any aspiring champion. Paradoxically, while entire libraries are devoted to the arcana of sub-variations, the answer to this profound question of the flesh has hitherto lain either undiscovered or deliberately concealed.

M y hypothesis is that sex is, indeed, within certain parameters, highly beneficial for one's chess. Given that the brain (which one would assume is useful for chess) is also the largest sex organ, one hopes this is not an obviously absurd proposition. It was one of my first girlfriends, Eva Stallings, who prompted the postulation that fornication was not only highly pleasurable to the senses, but also gainful to the Elo. I was just 19 years-old at the time. She was 32, German, and (unhappily) married to an older man in the United States. I had initially been introduced to her at the home of Frederic Friedel of ChessBase. We struck a warm rapport, and shortly afterwards she joined me in Esbjerg, Denmark, where I was playing a 12-player round-robin. Despite suffering a first-round loss, with White, to Michael Wiedenkeller, I nevertheless finished in clear first place, becoming the youngest GM in the world and the youngest ever from my country.

I t was not long before she accompanied me to the 1984 British Championship in Brighton. Again I suffered an early defeat, but little could stop my progress towards victory after I dispatched, among various others, my compatriot Tony Miles for the second time that summer. I thus became the youngest ever champion of my country. Those were halcyon seaside days of pink socks, t-shirts, a cheap B&B and a fun, energetic friend. I felt on top of the world.

I t was a while before I saw Eva again – in 1985, at the US-UK Challenge Match, against Lev Alburt, in Foxboro, Massachusetts. The organiser, Joel Altman, against whom I had previously played the only two correspondence games (two too many, I might add) of my entire life, had raised the funds notwithstanding a lack of support from the American Chess Foundation, who opined that I would be lucky to score half a point. They were almost right: I won 7-1, with Lev's habitual Alekhine Defence (perhaps a more appropriate choice for Opens than matches) providing little resistance.

U nfortunately, that was almost the last time I saw Eva (although we did meet briefly at a large simul I gave somewhere in Germany). Long-distance relationships are never easy and when we did meet, the passions were extremely intense. As a teenager, I didn't really have the maturity to handle it, to be honest.

I ncidentally, I learned, shortly after we first met, that Eva had been previously involved romantically with Bobby Fischer. She even became pregnant with his child but had decided, probably very wisely, that he was grossly unsuitable father-material. With great sadness, she chose a termination...

TO BOLDLY GO...

T he epilogue is that I found Eva on Facebook a while back. Her profile was, rather weirdly (and ominously with hindsight) full of pictures of fairies. We chatted affectionately about our times together and people in the chess world she had known. She promised to send me a photo of herself, but never did. I knew she had been unwell, but didn't realise quite how seriously that was. A short while later, an announcement appeared from her husband, on her page, saying that she had died.

W hat was it about Eva's tender presence that enabled me to score substantially in excess of my Elo rating? Of course, it is conceivable that my excellent results in her company were mere coincidence, but rather I doubt it. I would speculate it was more likely the surge of dopamine, from a surfeit of lovemaking, that inspired me to greater things (other neurotransmitters are also involved, but this is the main one).

H owever, as anyone who has ever experienced the excitement of a love-affair wearing off will know (intuitively, at least), dopamine levels remain elevated only for a few months, before falling back to their original level. If my hypothesis is correct, it would imply that for the right chemical stimulus to the brain a dedicated chess player would require a constant stream of new partners. This might make him a bit of a cad, but it would also optimise his results.

It is important to note though that visits to the whore-house are highly unlikely to bring a similar beneficent effect. A crude financial transaction and subsequent perfunctory coupling is, even if pleasantly tingling to the extremities, unequal to the suffusion of happiness attained by close amatory bonding with a new beau.

Before any of my priapic votaries rush out to explore their new licence, they should be aware of a most important caveat: in the introductory phase, sex often (although by no means necessarily) involves late nights and boozing, both of which are detrimental to one's chess. Sleep is so crucial to human beings that when starved of it we die with remarkable rapidity. Even mild sleep deprivation leads to impaired memory formation and other cognitive malfunctioning. Skimp on it at your extreme peril. Alcohol, while acting as a relaxant and increasing longevity in small doses, has the downside of dulling the thought-processes – not to mention also being addictive. Consumption thus tends to rise steadily over time, with increasingly adverse side-effects. Binge-drinking is even worse. Playing even partly under the influence with a throbbing hang-over is just an unmitigated disaster (and believe me – I have done it).

To consider how these various factors might conflict with each other, let's imagine a situation where a chess-playing paladin has invited the object of his affections, an attractive young lady, out to dinner. They talk, they laugh, they flirt, they hold hands, they even share a few glasses of wine. So far, so good. Then she suggests that they go to a bar. Here the first warning sign starts flashing. Had they immediately gone back to his or her room for cuddles, kisses and eventual rumpy-pumpy, all would have been well. But the new proposal inevitably means a late night (bad), with more alcohol being consumed (bad) and nor with guarantee of success (really bad). But he figures that the evening has been pleasant and that it would be churlish to decline, so they move to the next location. Hours pass by with more drinks being consumed. He now worries that while the erotically-tinged situation is not necessarily regressing, nor is it progressing in the desired horizontal

'Dare I again suggest that men and women have very different brains, without inviting howls of derision?'

direction. At what point should he, with an eye to the fast-approaching next round, abandon his lustful pursuit and retire to nurse his disappointment by sleeping alone in bed? Or should he gamble on a copulatory outcome, with potentially ruinous consequences? Not being a situation which lends itself to the easy application of a mathematical formula, it's a hard one to judge. These dilemmas do not occur in a stable relationship though. There, in essence, consent is the default option, so neither side need indulge in lengthy, elaborate courting-rituals.

The observant will have noticed this article has been written very much from a male perspective. It is germane to inquire whether this would equally apply to female chess players. Dare I again suggest that men and women have very different brains, without inviting howls of derision? Anyway, while not presenting these discussions as in any way definitive, I did ask a few female colleagues what they thought. The answers were broadly similar, but with some differences, in particular, a stronger emphasis on the emotional aspect. Yes, good sex and good chess tend to go hand in hand, but not always. 'Sometimes a dead bed and a good relationship is better', was one rueful comment.

The whole subject deserves proper academic scrutiny. For example, is ejaculation immediately prior to the game positive, or is the loss of energy of greater consequence? Intuitively I would assume that – as chess is not the most physical of sports – the upside would outweigh the down, but it would be interesting to know the answer definitively. My Guildford team-mate, the polymath David Smerdon, remarked that these days, particularly in the Netherlands, there is ample funding for such sex-based studies. Were he able to tap into those resources, he would be prepared, in a spirit of self-sacrifice, to undertake the research himself. Future generations will no doubt be grateful to the Australian Grandmaster for this pioneering work. However, knowing the meticulousness and scientific rigour with which he will undoubtedly undertake the task, there can be little danger of him publishing his conclusions soon. Completing field-studies and collating the results on such a pleasurable theme can be a very time-consuming business, as I am sure you can appreciate... ∎

LENNART OOTES

Congratulating the new champ is a good reason to briefly interrupt your game.

Caruana clinches title in US Championship debut

Nazi Paikidze springs upset in Women's Championship

Four-time Italian Champion Fabiano Caruana is the 2016 national champion of the country where he was born 23 years ago.

Boasting three GMs from the world's top 10, the 2016 US Championship was the strongest one in history. The expected three-man race between top-seed Fabiano Caruana, four-time champion Hikaru Nakamura and Wesley So was contested right down to the final stretch, but in the end, prodigal son Caruana, the predicted favourite, prevailed. **VARUZHAN AKOBIAN** reports from St. Louis.

C
ontinuing a rich and wonderful tradition that was started in 2009, the 2016 US Championship was once again held at the now world-famous Chess Club and Scholastic Center of St. Louis. The prize-fund was $190,000, and with, finally, all three American super GMs taking part, it was a special edition to look forward to. Interestingly, it was the debut in the US Championship for Miami-born Caruana. In his 'Italian years' he won the Italian Championship four times (in 2007, 2008, 2010 and 2011) but never before did he vie for the American title. Now that he has returned to play for the US Chess Federation, this seemed a most apt moment to do so.

As it was, Caruana, who ranks number one in the US and number two in the world, grabbed the initiative from his first game. The luck of the draw matched him with the author of these lines, and in his play I detected no sign of lingering disappointment over his performance in the recent Candidates' Tournament, where he narrowly missed the opportunity to qualify and challenge Magnus Carlsen for the world title.

Caruana opened with 1.e4 and I responded with the Scandinavian Defence; one of the oldest asymmetric defences, along with the French. I selected this particular defence because of my familiarity with it, having played

it regularly some 20 years ago. Also, during my preparations, I noticed that the databases contain very few games in which he had played against this variation of the Scandinavian Defence, which includes 2...♘f6. Finally, I had hoped to surprise him in the opening and believe I did, as evidenced by the 20-minute time advantage I enjoyed after about eight moves.

He may have consumed some of that time recalling the opening of his game against Magnus Carlsen in the sixth round of the 2014 Chess Olympiad, in which Carlsen played a different variation of the same defence. In that game, though, Caruana enjoyed a nice advantage out of the opening, although he eventually lost to the reigning World Champion, who may rightfully be described as his arch-rival.

In our game, however, Caruana's play was confident and impressive throughout. When he was White, many of his victories seemed almost effortless, including his games against me, Shankland and Onischuk. He won the tournament with 8½ out of 11 points, a clear point ahead of second place.

'Kamsky put a lot of pressure on White, but like a true champion, Caruana managed to hold a difficult position.'

In one game only was the 23-year-old ever in danger. This was in his penultimate-round match-up against Gata Kamsky. The former world championship contender played amazingly well as Black in that game, obtaining an excellent position and a large advantage in the endgame, almost defeating Caruana in his Rossolimo Variation of the Sicilian. A Caruana loss would have turned the tournament upside down. In that case, Nakamura and So would have caught him, and the final round, with all three players in contention, would have been still more intense.

Kamsky put a lot of pressure on White, but like a true champion, Caruana managed to hold a difficult position.

At the opening ceremony former world championship contender Gata Kamsky was inducted in the World Chess Hall of Fame.

LENNART OOTES

Caruana-Kamsky
St. Louis 2016 (10)
position after 36.g4

This is the crucial moment in the game, and perhaps in the tournament. If Kamsky had played correctly, he could have won this game and turned everything on its head. **36...♗xd7?** After 36...♗e6! 37.♖d4 ♖xa3 38.♘c5 ♗b3 39.♖d3 ♖a1+ 40.♔h2 ♗d1 Black would have had good winning chances. **37.♖xd7 ♖xh3 38.♖xa7! ♖xa3 39.g5!**

A strong move, fixing Black's pawns on the kingside. Although Black is up a pawn, he will be unable to progress to a win. The game ended in a draw after 60 moves.

Hikaru Nakamura had come to St. Louis to defend his title. He endured an especially tough fourth round, losing with Black against Caruana and bolstering the general perception that Caruana was unstoppable. Nakamura said in an interview that he had pressed Caruana as Black because he 'had to do something'. He likewise continued attacking in later rounds, pressing to catch his main rival, who was now the clear leader.

NOTES BY
Fabiano Caruana

SI 19.13 – B80
Fabiano Caruana
Hikaru Nakamura
St. Louis 2016 (4)

My win against Nakamura in Round 4 obviously went a long way towards determining overall tournament victory. I was prepared for a big fight, but was surprised to find out later that Hikaru considered this an almost must-win situation for himself, which it just wasn't so early in the tournament, of course.

1.e4 c5 2.♘f3 d6 3.d4 cxd4 4.♘xd4 ♘f6 5.♘c3 a6 6.f3 e6 7.♗e3 h5!?

The Najdorf didn't come as a huge surprise, since it has been a mainstay of Nakamura's repertoire for many years, but this rare line with ...h5 was unexpected. Black prevents g4, which makes developing White's attack less straightforward. On the other hand, Black's kingside has been weakened and his king will probably remain in the centre for a long time, so there is some degree of risk with this strategy.

8.a4

Not a great move, but I wanted to try something original. The main moves are 8.♕d2 and 8.♗c4.

8...♘c6 9.♗c4

Aiming for a sort of Scheveningen with 9.♗e2 also makes sense, but I wanted to play more aggressively.

9...♕c7 10.♕e2 ♗e7 11.0-0 ♘e5 12.♗b3 ♗d7

At this point I had a long think. Black will continue with ...♖c8 and ...♘c4, so I have a choice of bishops to trade. The one on b3 felt really nice, so I decided to go for: **13.f4 ♘eg4 14.♔h1 ♘xe3 15.♕xe3**

Black has gained the bishop pair, but I have plenty of counterplay with f4-f5, aiming to weaken Black's light squares.

15...♕c5?!

Nakamura criticized this decision after the game. The move looks natural and felt strong to me during the game, but perhaps he's right that Black loses a valuable tempo.
It was possible to castle immediately, when 15...0-0-0 16.f5 is hit by 16...d5!, and the queen on c7 is eyeing h2.

16.♖ad1 g6?!

This move really does seem like a waste of time, since it doesn't prevent me from playing f5 in the long run.
I was more worried about 16...h4!?, with the idea of playing ...♘h5-g3+ under the right circumstances.

17.♕e2

A good move, getting my queen out of the pin, preventing ...♘g4 ideas and preparing both e5 and f5.

17...0-0-0

Maybe Black should try 17...h4!?, with the following possible variation: 18.e5 dxe5 19.fxe5 ♘h5 20.♕f3 0-0 21.♕xb7 ♖a7 22.♕e4 ♘g7, and Black has some compensation for the pawn.

18.f5

18.e5 was suggested as a stronger move, but it didn't seem that clear to me during the game, and still doesn't now: 18...dxe5 19.fxe5 ♘g4 20.♖xf7 ♔b8, and although White is undoubtedly better, there are a lot of pitfalls to avoid.

18...e5

18...gxf5 19.exf5 e5 was a perfectly viable option: 20.♗xf7 exd4 21.♕xe7, and here I missed a move, and perhaps Nakamura as well: 21...♕e5! 22.♕xe5 dxe5 23.♘d5 ♘xd5 24.♗xd5 ♗xa4, and the endgame should be close to equal.

19.♘f3 gxf5

20.♘g5!

He may have overlooked this move. The knight comes to f7 with strong effect.

20.exf5 h4, with ...♘h5 and ...♗c6 coming, is just a mess.

20...f4

This move feels positionally correct. The pawn is going to cramp White's style from f4.

20...fxe4 would lead to an interesting position: 21.♖xf6!? (not the only move, but my intention during the game. 21.♘d5 is also possible: 21...♘xd5 22.♖xd5 ♕b4 23.♘xf7 ♖hf8 24.♘xd8 ♖xf1+ 25.♕xf1 ♔xd8, and White might be slightly

better, but the position remains double-edged) 21...♗g4 22.♕e1 ♗xf6 23.♘gxe4 ♕b4 24.♘xf6 ♗xd1 25.♕xd1.

ANALYSIS DIAGRAM

I thought White would be better in this type of position because the minor pieces look dominating, but Black is ahead in material and the game is objectively very unclear.

21.♖d3
A move that just feels correct. The rook gets out of the way of ...♗g4 and is threatening to swing to c3 or b3 in the future.
21.♘xf7 ♗g4 22.♖f3 ♗xf3 23.gxf3 was tempting, but after some thought I decided I could play for more. After 23...♔b8 24.♘xh8 ♖xh8 Black is probably okay.

21...♔b8
Natural and probably the best move practically speaking.
The computer recommends 21...♖df8 22.♘d5 (22.♘xf7 ♖h7 23.♘g5 ♖g7 24.♘e6 ♗xe6 25.♗xe6+ ♔b8 26.b4! is even stronger, and I doubt Black will last long from this position) 22...♘xd5 23.♗xd5, and here I stopped my calculation, but 23...♕a7!

apparently holds, although I think you would need particularly large cojones to play this. Even the basic 24.♘f3!? seems pretty troublesome for Black in the long run.
21...♗g4 22.♕d2 doesn't help Black's cause at all.
21...h4 was mentioned by the commentators after the game. The line continues 22.♘d5 ♘xd5 23.♗xd5 ♗xg5 24.♖c3 ♔b8 25.♖xc5 dxc5, and now I like the simple 26.h3. Black's king is far from safe.

22.♘xf7 h4!
The point; and an excellent one it is! Suddenly ...♘h5 and ...♘g3+ are in the air. I was still sorely missing my dark-squared bishop.

23.♘xh8
Inaccurate. I should've kept the tension, as my intuition told me (I need to listen more).

23.♕f2! avoids the ...d5 idea, because after 23...d5 24.♕xc5 ♗xc5 25.♘xd8 ♖xd8 26.♗xd5 Black's rook will be needed on h8 to prepare ...♘h5-g3!.
23...♖xh8 24.♕f2

24...♕b4??
The decisive blunder, and quite a surprising one, because it's obvious that Black should under no circumstances allow the knight swap and a bishop outpost on d5.
24...♕a5 was suggested by Nakamura and is playable, but worse for Black.
However, 24...d5!! was a fantastic opportunity for counterplay: 25.♗xd5 (25.♕xc5? ♗xc5 26.♗xd5 ♘h5! is a sucker punch, as Maurice Ashley would say) 25...♕xf2 (even a move like 25...♕c7!? deserves attention, although it's probably not enough for equality) 26.♖xf2 ♗c5 27.♖ff3 ♗g4 (27...♘h5 now leads

nowhere after 28.h3 ♘g3+ 29.♔h2) 28.h3 ♗xf3 29.gxf3, and White is a pawn up, but Black shouldn't have too many problems holding a draw.

25.♘d5 ♘xd5

25...♕xe4 is met, not by the primitive 26.♘xe7, but by 26.♘xf6! ♗xf6 27.♖xd6, winning a bishop.

26.♗xd5 ♗xa4?

Black could have lasted longer if he had avoided this bishop blunder, but the result is no longer in doubt. White is up an exchange, with the initiative to boot.

27.♖a3!

The move he had missed. The bishop is immobile and White plays c3 and b3, trapping the bishop.

27...h3

27...♗b5 28.♕b6! is a cute trick.

28.c3 ♕b5 29.b3 ♗h4 30.bxa4 ♕d3 31.g3

Black resigned, because 31...♗xg3 is met by the simple 32.♕f3! ♕d2 33.♖a2.

■ ■ ■

After a win in the 10th and penultimate round, Nakamura stated that he was still recovering from a somewhat disappointing performance in the Candidates' Tournament in Moscow and that he had, to that point, been playing only 'reasonably well'. In Round 10, he defeated Jeffrey Xiong in the only game the 15-year-old GM lost in the championship. This win allowed Nakamura to catch up with Wesley to share second place.

NOTES BY
Varuzhan Akobian

KI 81.2 – E60
**Hikaru Nakamura
Jeffery Xiong**
St. Louis 2016 (10)

1.d4 ♘f6 2.c4 g6 3.f3

This move is becoming the most challenging one against the Grünfeld Defence, and it's no surprise that Nakamura is using it in this must-win game in the penultimate round in his fight for the title.

3...♘c6

Avoiding all the main lines after 3...d5 4.cxd5 ♘xd5 5.e4 ♘b6 6.♘c3 ♗g7 7.♗e3. This position is currently very popular, with White usually scoring well.

4.d5 ♘e5 5.e4 d6 6.♘c3 ♗g7 7.♗e2 0-0 8.f4 ♘ed7 9.♗e3 e6 10.dxe6 fxe6 11.♘h3 ♕e7 12.0-0 b6

This is the first new move. In one previous game, Black opted for 12...e5. However, Nakamura was playing very quickly and confidently, and looked very well prepared.

13.♗f3 ♖b8 14.♕c2 ♗b7 15.♖ae1 White completes his development. He has a better position because of his space advantage. The main problem for Black is his lack of a clear plan, so that every move requires a lot of thinking.

15...♔h8 16.♘g5

16...♗h6?! This is a dubious move. Better is for Black to remove the knight from g5 with 16...h6 17.♘h3, and White is slightly better.

17.♘b5 Aggressive play by White, but stronger was 17.h4! ♗g7 18.f5!, with a dangerous attack.

LENNART OOTES

'A great talent, Jeffery Xiong represents the future of the US Olympic team.'

17...♗xg5?!
The white knight on g5 was annoying. Still, it is very dangerous for Black to lose the dark-squared bishop and open the f-file.

Better was 17...e5! 18.♘xc7 exf4 19.♗xf4 ♘e5 20.♘ce6 ♗xg5 21.♘xg5 h6 22.♘h3 g5 23.♗xe5 dxe5, and despite being a pawn down, Black has some compensation due to the fact that White's dark squares are a little weak.

18.fxg5 ♘e8 19.♘xa7

19...♘e5 A better try would have been 19...c6 to lock the knight on a7, when White is still much better after 20.♕b3!.

20.♗e2! A good move, opening up the f-file and keeping the bishop pair.

20...♖xf1+ 21.♖xf1 ♖a8 22.♘b5 ♖xa2 23.♘a3 ♕g7

24.♗d2!
Excellent. Transferring the bishop to c3, protecting the weak b2-pawn and creating threats on the diagonal.

24...♘c6 25.♗c3 ♘d4 26.♗d3! ♔g8
White's queen cannot be captured because this would allow a mate on f8, 26...♘xc2 27.♖f8 mate.

27.♕f2 c5 28.♗b1 ♖a1 29.♘c2 ♖xb1 30.♖xb1 ♗xe4 31.♘xd4 ♗xb1

32.♘f5!
A nice final touch, winning Black's queen because of the devastating knight check that is threatened on h6.

32...exf5 33.♗xg7 ♔xg7 34.♕e3
Black resigned.

An excellent attacking game by Nakamura, inflicting Xiong's first and only loss of the tournament.

■ ■ ■

Going into the final round, Nakamura and So were a half point behind Caruana. If Nakamura had prevailed in the final round against Ray Robson and if So had defeated Aleksandr Lenderman, it would have set up the possibility of a tie-break if Caruana drew with IM Akshat Chandra. However, Nakamura managed only a draw against Robson, who was undefeated in a fine tournament performance, and So also drew.

Wesley So had enjoyed an excellent start to the tournament. His first game, a win against Gata Kamsky that involved a piece sacrifice, was one of the shortest games, a near-miniature that ended on the 28th move. Needless to say, such a result against Kamsky is a rare occurrence indeed.

NOTES BY
Wesley So

RL 25.14 – C95
Wesley So
Gata Kamsky
St. Louis 2016 (1)

The 2016 US Championships! St. Louis, Missouri, Chess Capital of the World! I was looking at a long line of 29 games – 11 classical and 18 blitz in the ensuing Ultimate Blitz Challenge with Garry Kasparov. How would it all go? For me, Round 1 is usually the toughest game in an event and always poses philosophical questions. How will I do? Can I win that first one, or will I start with a draw (or worse, a loss)? For me, most of the time a strong start signals a good run ahead, so for this first game I was really hoping to do well, mentally weighing my chances. On the one hand, Gata Kamsky is a five-time US Champion, and during the opening ceremonies of this same event, he was inaugurated into the Chess Hall of Fame (along with fellow GM Maurice Ashley). That is a huge boost and would certainly mean extra energy

and motivation for him. On the other hand, Gata just got back from a series of (four) strong tournaments in Europe and it was a hopeful possibility that he might still be a little jet-lagged. Let's see what happened.
1.e4!
In the interview after the game Gata mentioned that he had been expecting 1.d4. But I was eager to meet his Breyer, or his Sicilian systems.
1...e5 Played after a few minutes of thought. **2.♘f3 ♘c6 3.♗b5 a6**
No Berlin today! Hurrah! I suppose Gata, having just returned from Germany, wanted to play something a bit more American.
4.♗a4 ♘f6 5.0-0 ♗e7 6.♖e1 b5 7.♗b3 d6 8.c3 0-0 9.h3 ♘b8

In the end, Gata decided to stick to what he knows the best: the Breyer Defence. This solid system was first introduced by Gyula Breyer back in 1911, and it gives Black flexibility and good coordination for his pieces. The only downside is that it gives White a space advantage.
10.d4 ♘bd7 11.♘bd2 ♗b7 12.♗c2

12...♖e8

12...c5 is always met by 13.d5!, when the bishop on b7 is staring at a concrete pawn wall.
13.♘f1 ♗f8 14.♘g3 g6 15.♗g5 Provoking Black to weaken his kingside a little bit.
15...h6 If 15...♗g7 then 16.♕d2 will yield White some nicely placed pieces. **16.♗d2** Not the best place for the bishop, but White has to keep the e4-pawn protected.
It does not make sense to give up the bishop pair unnecessarily with 16.♗e3 exd4 17.♗xd4 c5 18.♗xf6 ♘xf6.
16...♗g7 17.a4

17...c6 I think Gata wanted to play solidly, while at the same time avoiding the main theoretical paths.
17...c5 is the main move, upon which I had based my main preparation: 18.d5 c4 19.b4 cxb3 20.♗xb3 ♘c5 21.c4.

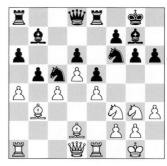

ANALYSIS DIAGRAM

Adams recently defended this comfortably with Black against Vachier-Lagrave, but I believe White can exert pressure. The main issue is that Black's bishops are not well-placed, and the d6-pawn can become vulnerable. I suppose a good technical player would be able to play this position well with both colours.

17...♘b6 is what Pavel Eljanov recommends in his recent repertoire DVD *The Ruy Lopez Breyer Variation*. This is a good starting point for players who are eager to learn more about this complex opening and who want the insights of a top GM. This might be fine (and the best move) for Black, although the lines can get concrete and good preparation is needed. The idea is that 18.b3 bxa4 19.bxa4 a5

ANALYSIS DIAGRAM

gives Black a good grip on the queenside, and a well-placed knight on b6.

'I suppose Gata, having just returned from Germany, wanted to play something a bit more American.'

His analysis continues 20.♗d3 ♕c8 21.d5 c6 22.♖b1 ♘bd7 23.c4 ♘c5 24.♗e3 ♘fd7, with an equal position, as White's pawns can get weak, too.

18.axb5 I wanted to clarify the situation in order to see which pawn he was going to recapture with.

The alternative is 18.♗d3 ♕c7 19.♕c1 ♔h7, which looks more pleasant for White. The problem is that he

will have to select a plan from the many choices he has. Should he play on the queenside or on the kingside? Personally I might consider ♘h4-f5 or h4-h5...

18...axb5

18...cxb5 is, I believe, a more complex recapture. After 19.d5 ♖c8 20.♗d3 ♘c5 (20...♘b6 21.b3) 21.♗f1 White should be better because he has more space, but there's a long game ahead.

19.♖xa8

19...♕xa8

19...♗xa8, which Gata suggested later, might be better, as it discourages ♘h4 ideas. In this case I might have had to play more slowly: 20.♗e3, with the idea of ♕d2, then ♖d1 to improve my piece placement, and later fighting for control of the d-file.

20.♘h4

Some people thought that I simply caught Gata in a deeply-prepared line, but this is not the case. I found this ♘h4-f5 idea over the board! I just wanted to attack as fast as I could. For this game my blitzkrieg tactics worked well!

20...♕d8?!

An attack on the flank is best met by a counter-attack in the centre! Using this formula, one can conclude that the best move for Black is 20...exd4! 21.cxd4 c5 22.d5 ♕d8, and now White might have to retreat his forces for a bit, starting with 23.♘f3 (23.♘hf5 gxf5 24.♘xf5 ♘e5 25.♘xh6+ ♗xh6 26.♗xh6 ♘h7 does not look very clear).

The other way to open the centre is not as effective: 20...d5 21.dxe5! ♘xe5 22.f4 ♘c4 23.e5 ♘e4 24.♘xe4 dxe4 25.♗c1

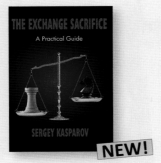

ANALYSIS DIAGRAM

The analysis should not stop here, but I'll leave it to the reader to assess the position.

20...c5 is again met by 21.d5.

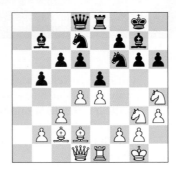

21.♕c1! ♔h7? This basically forces White to sacrifice a piece.

Black's best was 21...♘h7! 22.♘f3 (22.♘hf5 gxf5 23.♘xf5 ♖e6 looks unclear, as Black's rook defends d6, h6, and the third rank, basically keeping his position together) 22...h5, and now White can choose between 23.♗h6 or 23.♖d1, in both cases with a pleasant position.

22.♘hf5! I didn't even hesitate. Sacrificing one knight gets me a powerful knight on f5, at least a couple of pawns, and a vulnerable king to

attack. You couldn't hope for a better opportunity!
22...gxf5 23.♘xf5

23...♖e6

23...♘g8 24.♘xd6 reminds me of a famous Kasparov-Karpov game, which I suppose every serious chess player knows, the second game of their match in New York in 1990.

Kasparov-Karpov
New York 1990 (m-2)
position after 24...♘g8

25.♗xh6! ♗xh6 26.♘xh6 ♘xh6 27.♘xd6 ♕b6 28.♘xe8 ♕xd4+ 29.♔h1 ♕d8 30.♖d1 ♕xe8 31.♕g5 ♖a7 32.♖d8 ♕e6 33.f4 ♗a6 34.f5 ♕e7 35.♕d2 ♕e5 36.♕f2 ♕e7 37.♕d4 ♘g8 38.e5 ♘d5 39.fxg6+ fxg6 40.♖xc6 ♕xd8 41.♕xa7+ ♘de7 42.♖xa6 ♕d1+ 43.♕g1 ♕d2 44.♕f1 1-0.

24.♗xh6

I took some time to make this move, as 24.d5 looked very tempting.

After 24.d5 cxd5 25.exd5 ♘xd5 White has a pleasing discovered check, but surprisingly it doesn't lead to much: 26.♘xd6+ (or 26.♘xh6+ ♔g6 27.♘xf7 ♕f6) 26...♔g8 27.♘xb7 ♕c7 28.♗f5, and White still has a large advantage, although smaller than I wanted.

24...♞e8 24...♝h8 is met by 25.d5 and 24...♞h5 by 25.♝g5. **25.♝g5**

25...♝f6? 25...♛b6 might be the best defence. Still White's position is very easy to play: 26.d5 ♖g6 27.dxc6 ♝xc6 28.♝b3, and f7 is too weak. After 25...f6 26.♝h6 ♚g8 27.♖e3, Black also has too many holes in his position.
26.♝xf6 ♛xf6 White also wins after 26...♖xf6 27.♛g5 ♛a5 28.♝b3.
27.d5

27...♖e7 Or 27...cxd5 28.exd5 ♝xd5 29.♞e7+. **28.g4** Maybe Gata had overlooked this. Black resigned, because there is no way to defend the e7-rook. So my tournament had got off to a good start!

■ ■ ■

In Round 5 our reporter Varuzhan Akobian ran into the deep opening preparation of a fast playing Wesley So.

Wesley So had a solid tournament, with none of the distractions that had hampered his performance in the previous year. And he was well-prepared against sharp lines, as he demonstrated in his game against me. However, by the end, he had made too many draws as White, including one against Robson, his former college roommate. 'You can call me an underdog,' So said. 'Everyone here just wants to give their best and let's see what happens.' Against the strongest field of contenders ever to compete at the US Championship, those draws prevented him from catching Caruana and fighting for the title. This is what happened in our game:

FR 7.4 – C10
Wesley So
Varuzhan Akobian
St. Louis 2016 (5)

1.e4 e6 2.d4 d5 3.♞c3 dxe4
I chose the Rubinstein Variation to obtain a solid position, but ran into excellent preparation by Wesley So.

4.♞xe4 ♞d7 5.♞f3 ♞gf6 6.♞xf6+ ♞xf6 7.c3

As So mentioned after the game, this move was played by Kasparov against Ponomariov in the 2002 Linares super-tournament, where White won a nice game.
7...c5 8.♝e3

8...cxd4?! My first mistake of the game. I should have stuck with the main theory, which I knew but hadn't reviewed before the game. I made a draw in this line against former FIDE World Champion Ruslan Ponomariov as Black at the 2009 World Cup. So had probably prepared something interesting.
8...♛c7 9.♞e5 a6 10.♛a4+ ♞d7 11.♝b5 cxd4 12.♝xd7+ ♝xd7 13.♛xd4 ♝b5 14.a4 ♝d6 15.♞xf7 ♚xf7 16.axb5 axb5 was my game against Ponomariov.
9.♝xd4 ♝e7 10.♝d3 0-0 11.♛c2
My opponent was playing very quickly and I realized he was well prepared. My position is worse, since he has two strong bishops and a clear plan to attack my king after castling queenside.
11...h6 12.0-0-0 ♛a5 13.♚b1

NEW IN CHESS bestsellers

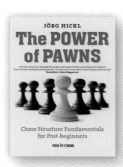

The Power of Pawns
Chess Structures Fundamentals for Post-Beginners
Jörg Hickl   192 pages - €18.95

"The didactic concept of the book is admirable. Each chapter defines the structures, explains the typical characteristics and shows the plans for both White and Black. The reader participates by assessing positions and invariably receives useful tips for practical play." – *Harry Schaack, KARL magazine*

"There are lots of valuable training lessons, in particular in areas where chess engines offer no help." *Harald Fietz, SchachMagazin 64*

A Chess Opening Repertoire for Blitz and Rapid
Sharp, Surprising and Forcing Lines for Black and White
Evgeny & Vladimir Sveshnikov 416 pages - €27.95

A repertoire for club players that is forcing, both narrow and deep, and aggressive.

"There is lots of analyis AND lots of explanatory text." Dennis Monokroussos, The Chess Mind

"The whole project is such a clever idea: Why hadn't anyone else thought of this before?" – *GM Glenn Flear*

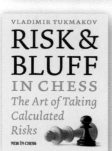

Mastering Chess Middlegames
Lectures from the All-Russian School of Grandmasters
Alexander Panchenko   272 pages - €22.95

"The deeper I went into the book, the more fresh and fascinating material I found."
Sean March, CHESS Magazine

"A very systematic way of looking at chess middlegames. Extremely instructive, with many fresh examples." *GM Daniel King*

The Lazy Man's Sicilian
Attack and Surprise White with the Basman-Sale Variation
Valeri Bronznik & Steve Giddins 208 pages - €19.95

Surprising, aggressive and easy to learn: after the normal moves 1.e4 c5 2.Nf3 e6 3.d4 cxd4 4.Nxd4 Black lashes out with 4...Bc5!. Ideal for players who don't have much time to study theory (or are not too fond of hard work).

"A very good book which offers a relatively simple Sicilian system." – *IM Dirk Schuh, Rochade Europa*

Risk & Bluff in Chess
The Art of Taking Calculated Risks
Vladimir Tukmakov   224 pages - €24.95

After studying this book, you will think twice before wasting an opportunity to do what the greatest players do: bluff your way to victory!

"Risk & Bluff is fantastic" – *Jeremy Silman*

"Probably the most recommendable middlegame book of the year." – *British Chess Magazine*

100 Endgames You Must Know
Vital Lessons for Every Chess Player
Jesus de la Villa   254 pages - €22.95

"If you've never read an endgame book before, this is the one you should start with."
GM Matthew Sadler, former British Champion

"If you really have no patience for endgames, at least read 100 Endgames You Must Know."
Gary Walters Chess

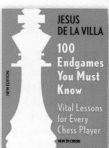

The Double Queen's Gambit
A Surprise Weapon for Black
Alexey Bezgodov   272 pages - €24.95

Former Russian Chess Champion Alexey Bezgodov provides a complete repertoire for Black against 1.d4, starting with the cheeky move 2...c5! against both 2.c4 and 2.♘f3.

"Maybe it isn't so easy for White to prove a large advantage here and the line will almost certainly surprise your opponent." *CHESS Magazine*

Bologan's Ruy Lopez for Black
How to Play for a Win against the Spanish Opening
Victor Bologan   544 pages - €29.95

"A shortcut to success against the Ruy Lopez."
IM Gary Lane, Chess Moves Magazine

"Essential reading."
Kanwal Bhatia, CHESS Magazine

"A fantastic book, just as 'Bologan's Black Weapons' was. A complete repertoire full of surprising ideas."
FM Richard Vedder, Schakers.info

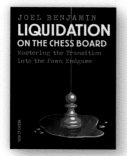

Liquidation on the Chess Board
Mastering the Transition into the Pawn Ending
Joel Benjamin   256 pages - €19.95

WINNER: 2015 Best Book Award, Chess Journalists of America (CJA)
SHORTLISTED: English Chess Federation 2015 Book of the Year

"An excellent guide to a difficult theme that has been badly served in chess literature. If you are really serious about improving your chess, you should work on your Benjamin!"
IM Frank Zeller, Magazine Schach

The Even More Flexible French
Strategic Ideas & Powerful Weapons
Viktor Moskalenko   304 pages - €26.95

"Moskalenko does an excellent job of explaining what Black is aiming for and the 103 model games this book is structured around make it more user friendly for amateur players than the traditional opening book." – *IM John Donaldson*

"All French players wishing to refresh their repertoire should examine this work, both for new ideas in the main lines and some tricky surprise weapons." – *CHESS Magazine*

available at your local (chess)bookseller or at www.newinchess.com

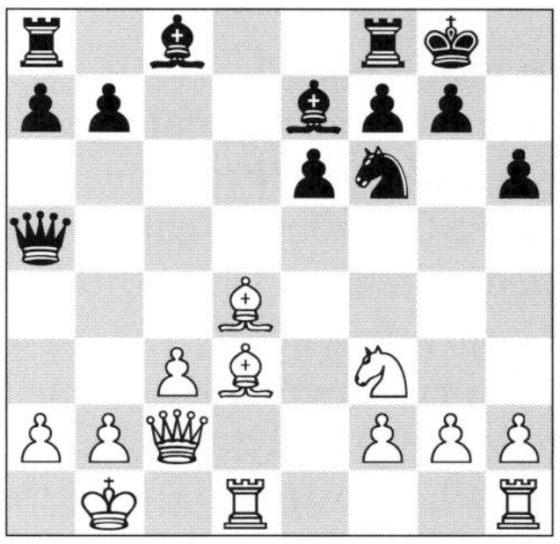

13...♖d8 My best move here is 13...b5 14.♗e4 ♖b8 15.♘e5 (15.♗e5 won't work because of the clever reply 15...♗b7, when 16.♗xb8 fails to 16...♗xe4) 15...♗b7 16.♗xb7 ♖xb7 17.f4, when White is only slightly better.

14.♘e5 ♗d7

I was hoping that my opponent would capture my light-squared bishop, giving him a slight advantage but still leaving me with a solid and playable position.

15.♕e2

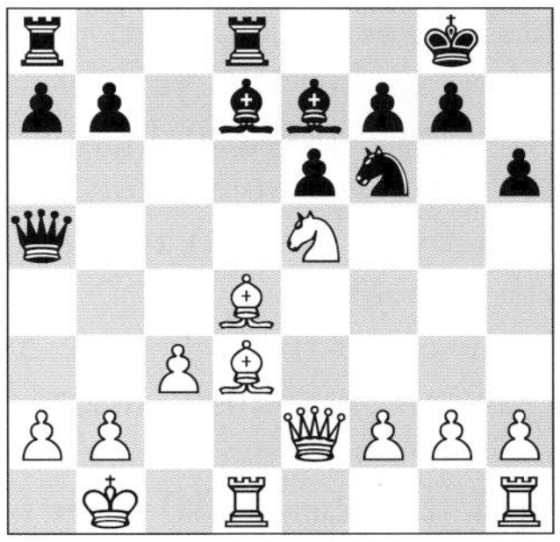

15...♗c6 Perhaps I should have gone 15...♗a4 16.♖de1 ♗c6 17.♖hg1 ♖xd4 18.cxd4 ♗d5, when Black is down an exchange, but most importantly, White no longer has a dangerous attack.

16.♖he1 ♗d5 I should still have sacrificed the exchange on d4, 16...♖xd4 17.cxd4 ♗d5, which would have been my best practical chance.

17.c4

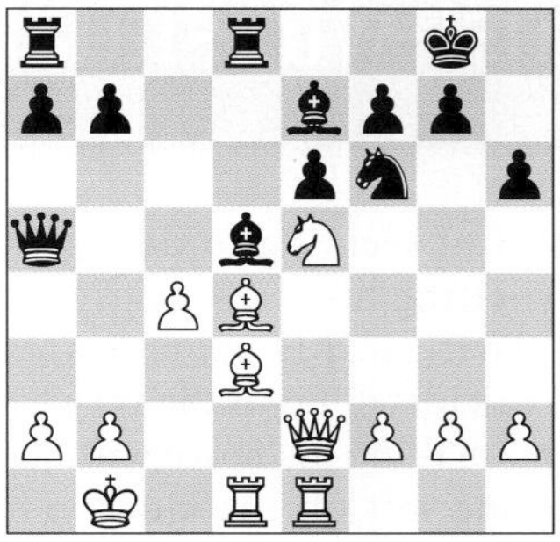

17...♗xg2 This looks very dangerous, but I didn't have a choice. If I play 17...♗c6, White has 18.♘xf7! (or 18.♗c3 ♕c7 19.f4 ♗e8 20.g4, with a strong attack) 18...♖xd4 19.♕xe6 ♖xd3 20.♖xd3 ♕xe1+ 21.♕xe1 ♔xf7 22.f3, with a large advantage for White.

18.♗c3

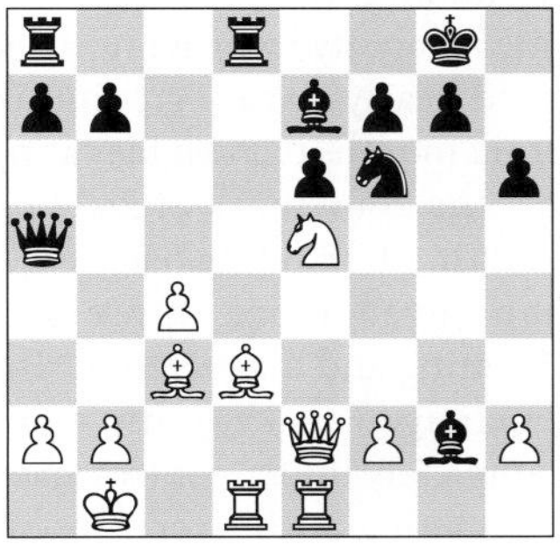

18...♕b6?

I really regret playing this move after spending all my time (about 30 minutes). I should have trusted my intuition and gone for 18...♗b4 19.♘xf7 ♖xd3! 20.♘xh6+ ♔h8 21.♖xd3 (or 21.♗xf6 ♖xd1+ 22.♖xd1 gxf6 23.♖d4 ♖e8! 24.♕g4 ♔h7 25.♕xg2 ♖d8 26.♕h3 ♖xd4 27.♘f5+ ♔g6 28.♘xd4 ♕e5, and here too, White is only slightly better) 21...♗xc3 22.♖xc3 ♗e4+ 23.♔a1 gxh6 24.♕d2 ♕g5, when White is only slightly better.

19.♖g1

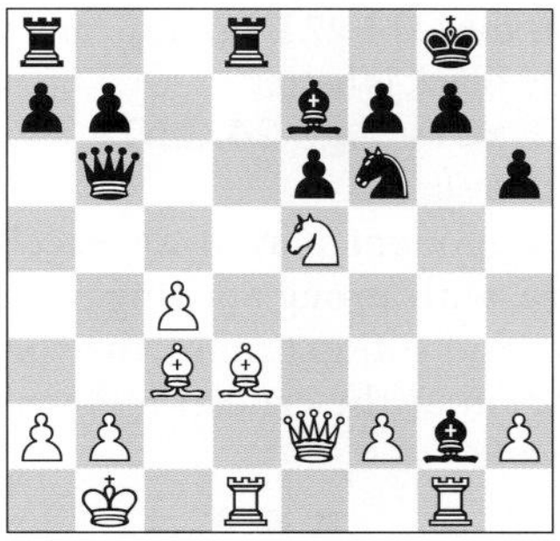

19...♗c6

I should have tried 19...♖xd3 20.♘xd3 ♕c6 21.♘e5 ♕e4+ 22.♕xe4 ♗xe4+ 23.♔a1, when White is clearly better, but Black has some fighting chances.

20.♘xf7!

So finds a beautiful tactical combination involving various sacrifices.

20...♔xf7

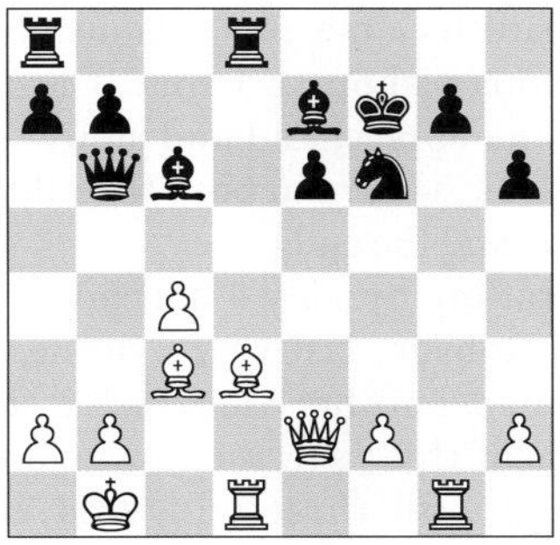

21.♖xg7+! ♔xg7 22.♕xe6 ♕xf2

This move loses immediately. My only chance was to try 22...♖e8! 23.♖g1+ ♔f8 24.♕f5! (only this one) 24...♗g2 25.♖xg2 ♖ad8 26.♕g6, and White is giving mate.

I had seen 24.♗xf6?

St. Louis 2016 — cat. XVII

					1	2	3	4	5	6	7	8	9	10	11	12		TPR
1	Fabiano Caruana	IGM	USA	2795	*	½	1	½	1	½	½	1	1	1	½	1	8½	2854
2	Wesley So	IGM	USA	2773	½	*	½	½	½	½	1	½	½	1	1	1	7½	2778
3	Hikaru Nakamura	IGM	USA	2787	0	½	*	½	½	1	½	1	1	1	1	½	7½	2777
4	Ray Robson	IGM	USA	2663	½	½	½	*	1	½	½	½	½	½	1	1	7	2757
5	Alexander Onischuk	IGM	USA	2664	0	½	½	0	*	½	½	1	1	½	½	1	6	2691
6	Jeffery Xiong	IGM	USA	2618	½	½	0	½	½	*	1	½	½	½	½	½	5½	2659
7	Gata Kamsky	IGM	USA	2678	½	0	½	½	½	0	*	½	½	½	½	1	5	2618
8	Samuel Shankland	IGM	USA	2656	0	½	0	½	0	½	½	*	½	1	0	1	4½	2591
9	Aleksandr Lenderman	IGM	USA	2618	0	½	0	½	0	½	½	½	*	½	½	1	4½	2594
10	Varuzhan Akobian	IGM	USA	2615	0	0	0	½	½	½	½	0	½	*	1	1	4½	2594
11	Alexander Shabalov	IGM	USA	2528	½	0	0	0	½	½	½	1	½	0	*	½	4	2565
12	Akshat Chandra	IM	USA	2477	0	0	½	0	0	½	0	0	0	0	½	*	1½	2363

ANALYSIS DIAGRAM

and I thought I would get mated by ♖g8, but I missed an amazing defensive move: 24...♗g2!! 25.♗xe7+ ♖xe7 26.♕xb6 axb6 27.♖xg2 ♖g7, and suddenly Black is better.
23.♕xe7+ ♔g8 24.♗h7+
Black resigned.
My opponent played an excellent game, with strong opening preparation, and I didn't make the correct decision at the crucial moment on move 18.

∎ ∎ ∎

In the final round, playing as Black, Caruana was not about to allow 16-year-old Akshat Chandra, the lowest-rated of the contenders, to be a spoiler. It should be noted that Chandra had two GM norms at the time of the event. Chandra played well in the opening, and forced the leader to demonstrate his reputation for exact and thorough calculation in a Spanish Game. But after an advantageous bishop exchange, Caruana got the upper hand and slowly outplayed Chandra in both the middlegame and the endgame.

Trailing by only a half point was Ray Robson, last year's runner-up. He had another impressive tournament this year, remaining undefeated with three wins and eight draws. He inserted himself into the mix from the beginning and almost managed to make it a four-man contest, as Nakamura had predicted might happen at the beginning of the tournament.

Robson performed particularly well under time-pressure, even to

the point of seeming to defy pressure by letting his clock nearly run down. Twice in his game against me, he calculated up to the very last moment, making his move with just one second left on the clock. The only player plagued with more time-trouble during the tournament was Chandra.

Jefferey Xiong, only 15 years old and the tournament's only wild card pick, had a very impressive showing in his first US Championship, finishing sixth out of a field of 12 players, with one win (against Kamsky), one loss (to Nakamura), and nine draws. His game is rapidly improving, as he has earned nearly 50 rating points in the past six months to push his rating well past the 2600 mark at 2624 on the May 2016 FIDE rating list.

Perhaps even more impressive than his rating and his meteoric rise, Xiong managed to keep his emotions completely under control, even while competing in this very important and high-pressure event. For his age, he is very composed, virtually never standing up during his games to peruse other people's games or for any other reason. He appears to be an exceptionally focused player and a tough fighter, tenacious, calculating, and especially creative in defence.

A great talent, Xiong represents the future of the US Olympic team. And his talent is superseded only by his humility. About his win against GM Kamsky he said: 'It's nothing really about the opponent. I just think that lately I've been very lucky against him... extremely lucky.'

> **'Ferocious' is the word Irina Krush used to describe Paikidze's play as Black in the must-win situation.**

Pure Hollywood

If the men's tournament was a race between the top three tournament seeds, the US Women's championship seemed more like a Hollywood movie with a surprise ending. The competition was riveting, with a strong field that also included Anna Zatonskih again, who returned after a year's absence to compete for the title and resume her rivalry with Irina Krush.

Most of the drama occurred in the 11th and final round. Tatev Abrahamyan, who had been the tournament leader for most of the event and who was leading by a half point going into that final round, underestimated her 15-year-old opponent Ashritha Eswaran, the US Junior Girls' Champion. Abrahamyan played the Sicilian Najdorf instead of her usual French Defence against her younger opponent's 1.e4, intending to 'muddy the waters'. However, Eswaran was well prepared against this variation and played a great positional game. The leader soon stumbled, found herself in a losing position and resigned shortly thereafter.

This was not the only time Abrahamyan came extremely close to winning this event. Given that she has come so very close on so many occasions, it appears to be simply a matter of time before she wins her first US Women's Championship title.

Spectators could not have hoped for a more exciting match-up in the final round, in which seven-time champion Irina Krush played Nazi Paikidze. This year, Paikidze competed in what was only her second US Women's Championship. She was undefeated in the 2015 event, in which she finished in second place. She was likewise undefeated in this tournament and became its champion. She managed to find sharp continuations that overwhelmed Krush, spectacularly complicating the game to win the title. 'Ferocious' is the word Irina Krush used to describe Paikidze's play as Black in the must-win situation.

Indeed, throughout the entire tournament, it's difficult to find a position in which Paikidze appears to be in any sort of trouble, and in some of the games she drew, she had enjoyed positions that were simply winning. In my opinion, and one shared by several other players in the tournament, Paikidze played the best chess in the US Women's Championship and deservedly won the title.

Let's finish with the Hollywood drama that I already mentioned, described in the new champion's own words.

NOTES BY
Nazi Paikidze

RE 26.13 – A07
Irina Krush
Nazi Paikidze
St. Louis 2016 (11)

If I had been hoping for a finish that would clinch me first place, things were not looking very promising when I was going into the final round. To begin with, I was a half point behind the leader, Tatev Abrahamyan. In her last game, Tatev was facing off against the young and less experienced Ashritha Eswaran. In previous matches, Tatev had completely dominated Ashritha, whereas I had been paired as Black with the seven-time champion Irina Krush. I absolutely needed a win, since this would help improve my chances of getting to a playoff if Tatev were to draw her game. It was a long shot, but I had to do everything in my power to give myself a run at first place. Additionally, because Tatev and I had separated ourselves from the rest of the field, we had secured 1st and 2nd place, regardless of the other results. Managing to qualify for the playoffs was already a dream result. I did not, even for a second, consider another scenario: that if I won my game and Tatev lost hers, I would be champion

after the last round. I knew what I had to do. My hopes were on the playoffs, for which I absolutely had to beat Irina Krush. My strategy was to get into a complicated position from the opening and prepare for a long fight. Irina was also looking for a win in the last round, to come back after a surprising loss against the youngest player in the championship, Carissa Yip.

1.♘f3 ♘f6 2.g3

I was expecting something sharper and more ambitious in the opening. I admit that I was disappointed at this point, thinking we would get a quiet, positional game.

2...d5 3.♗g2 c6 4.0-0 ♗g4 5.d3 ♘bd7

6.h3 6.♘bd2 is the main line, with thousands of games in the database.
6...♗h5 7.♕e1 e5 8.e4 dxe4 9.dxe4 ♗c5 My theoretical knowledge in this opening officially ended here. I had never played this variation with Black, but then again, no one has ever played this opening with White against me either.
10.a4 a5 11.♘a3

Irina made all her first 11 moves very quickly. It was obvious that she had prepared this position, whereas I was seeing it for the first time.
11...0-0 12.♘c4 ♕c7 13.♗d2 b6 14.♘h4 ♖fe8 15.♔h1 ♗g6
So far, all the moves seemed clear.
16.♘xg6

Nazi Paikidze: 'My strategy was to get into a complicated position from the opening and prepare for a long fight.'

clearly better) 23.♗xc8 ♖xf1+ 24.♖xf1 ♖xc8, and after all this madness, we are left with an equal endgame.

At the board I only saw 21...♘f6, thinking it was a good option for Black. However, I missed a winning idea for White: 21...♘f6?? 22.♗xa8 ♖xe1 23.♗xe1!. This is a strong move, keeping all the white pieces defended.

– Finally, after 18.♘xa5?! exf4 White can't recapture on f4 with any of the three pieces:

19.♖xf4 ♘h5 20.♖f3 ♘df6, and White's position is falling apart.

19.♗xf4?? ♕xa5.

19.gxf4? ♘xe4! 20.♗xe4 ♘f6.

18...♕c8! I had a major decision to make here: ...♕b8 or ...♕c8. The text-move keeps an eye on the h3-pawn.

I could not find anything wrong with ...♕b8, but it would lead to many exchanges and simplify the position too much for Black to try and fight for a win: 18...♕b8 19.♘xe5 ♘xe5 20.fxe5 ♕xe5 21.♗c3 ♗d4, with an equal position.

19.axb5

According to my database, this is a novelty, which is not too surprising, since only a couple of games had been played with this line.

16...hxg6 17.f4

I was happy to see this move. Instead of 'boring' positional play (♕e2, ♖d1, c3, etc.), Irina chose a more aggressive continuation. I knew this was my chance to create chaos on the board.

transposes to what happened in the game). I saw that I would have enough compensation after 19...♗b6, as Black is going to get the sacrificed pawn back (c2). But I also had another option that could lead to many interesting lines: 19...exf4 20.gxf4 (20.♖xf4? is a mistake in view of 20...♘h5) 20...♘xe4 21.♗xe4

ANALYSIS DIAGRAM

17...b5! To be honest, I did not calculate all the possible continuations after 17...b5. This move was made mostly by a combination of intuition and the 'must-win' situation of this particular match.

18.♗xa5 However, I am not the type of player who likes 'winging it', so I did calculate the following variations:

– 18.axb5 cxb5 19.♘xa5 (19.♗xa5

21...♕c8!!. A computer move, threatening ...♘f6 and checkmate on h3: 22.♗b7! (after 22.♔h2 ♘f6 23.♗xa8 ♖xe1 24.♗xe1 ♕xa8, White materially has enough compensation for the queen. However, Black's position is preferable due to White's weaknesses on the kingside) 22...♖xe1 (only this move, as after 22...♕b8? 23.♕g3 ♖xa5 24.♗xa5 ♕xb7+ 25.♕f3 White is

19...cxb5

Unfortunately, I spent a lot of time here calculating what turned out to be a losing move for Black: 19...exf4?? 20.bxc6 f3 21.♖xf3! (21.cxd7? fxg2+ 22.♔xg2 ♛xd7; 21.♗xf3?? ♘e5) 21...♛xc6 22.e5!.

I am glad I did not go for this disaster.

20.♘d2

I was expecting 20.♘xe5 ♘xe5 21.fxe5 ♖xe5 and I liked this position for Black. There was definitely good compensation for the pawn: the weak e4-pawn and the somewhat weak king on h1. White has to be careful and I could not find a good continuation for her: 22.♛e2 (22.♗c3?! ♖xa1 23.♛xa1 ♖h5! 24.h4 ♘g4; 22.♔h2?? ♘g4+! 23.hxg4 ♛xg4 24.♗h1 ♖h5+ 25.♔g2 ♛h3+ 26.♔f3 ♖g5) 22...♘xe4.

20...exf4 21.gxf4

21.♖xf4? runs into 21...♗d6.

21...♘d5!

I was quite happy when I saw this move. It is not only beautiful, but also very strong. The black knight is heading for e3 to make the white pieces extremely uncomfortable.

22.♖f3

After 22.e5 ♘e3 I was not afraid to give up my rook for the g2-bishop: 23.♗xa8 ♛xa8+ 24.♘f3 ♘xc2.

22...f5!?

I spent less than a minute on this move. It seemed like an obvious and correct continuation for Black. However, if I had spent more time in this sharp position, I would have realized that ...f5 seriously weakens my king and was unnecessary.

A better move was 22...♘7f6, heading for h5, with a large positional advantage.

23.e5

This seemed a natural reaction to ...f5, but White had something much stronger: 23.♛e2! is a very simple, yet hard to find move. White improves the queen's position and attacks the b5-pawn. Also, it is a great 'waiting move', as it is not easy for Black to find a good move afterward. For instance, 23...fxe4 (or 23...♘7f6 24.e5 ♘h5 25.♛xb5 ♘dxf4 26.♛c4+, with great counterplay for White. Now you can clearly see the weakness created by 22...f5) 24.♘xe4, when Black's king is exposed and White's position is far better. This would have been a really strong continuation for White.

23...g5!

This was the second time in the championship that I made a strong pawn move to g5 (the first instance being in the game Yip-Paikidze). I call it my move of the tournament. I saw Irina's reaction to it – she looked surprised, confused and a little worried. I felt confident. I was about to deconstruct the centre and my pieces were ready to get closer to her king.

This was the first time in the game that I felt that I could win.

24.fxg5?!

Best was 24.b4!. Again, a computer move. The idea of 24.b4 is to make Black's strong bishop leave the g1-a7 diagonal and it is worth blocking her bishop on a5. Now, after 24...♗d4? (after 24...♗f8 25.♕d1! the knight on d5 is hanging and it is difficult to defend it. This is a very dangerous position for Black) 25.c3! ♗xc3 (25...♘xc3?? 26.♘b3; 25...♗a7

'I call it my move of the tournament. I saw Irina's reaction to it – she looked surprised, confused and a little worried.'

26.♕d1!) 26.♖c1 all the black pieces are terrible and the king is going to be in a lot of danger very quickly.

24...♘xe5

I loved looking at my great knights and strong bishop! Saying this is a pleasant position for Black would be very modest.

25.♖f2??

A big mistake. But White already did not have anything too great.
After 25.♖f1, 25...♘e3 is pretty uncomfortable.

25...♘e3

I went for the safest continuation.
I spent about 30 minutes calculating the obvious move, 25...♘d3. It appeared to be winning... It felt it had to be winning, but I could not back it up with a variation. I must admit that deliberately leaving a piece hanging with a check was not an easy thing to do, especially true in the most important game of your life to date! Where to put my king?
After 25...♘d3! 26.♗xd5+ I briefly

The old champion, Irina Krush, congratulates the new champion, Nazi Paikidze. 'Words cannot describe the relief and happiness I felt in that very moment.'

considered moving it to h8, but I was terrified of somehow getting checkmated. The engines, of course, are laughing: 26...♔h8! 27.♕xe8+ ♕xe8 28.♖xf5. At the board I thought White had enough compensation for the queen, with a rook, bishop, two pawns, my exposed king, plus a hanging knight and rook. I was very wrong. Black has at least two winning continuations:

ANALYSIS DIAGRAM

28...♕e3 29.♖f3 ♖xa5!! 30.♖xa5 ♕g1 mate. Or 28...♘f2+ 29.♖xf2 ♗xf2 30.♗xa8 ♕xa8+ 31.♔h2 ♕b8+ 32.♔h1 ♕g3, winning.

Again, being a human (and not a chess engine), I felt that moving my king to f8 seemed much more natural than moving it to the h-file. But I saw that this move would lose: 26...♔f8?? 27.♕xe8+! ♕xe8 (27...♔xe8 28.♖e2+!) 28.♖xf5+ ♔e7 29.cxd3.

A rook, two pieces, two pawns and a winning position for just one sad queen.

26.♘b3

Right at this moment, I saw Tatev Abrahamyan resign to her opponent. I realized that I only needed a draw to make it to the playoffs for the title. But if I won, I would immediately be champion. I have never felt so many emotions at the same time: shock, excitement, happiness, nervousness and impatience. I knew I had to calm down and hold it together in order to not let this opportunity slip away.

26...♘xg2

I went for the plan that I saw when I played 21...♘d5. But I missed another easy win: 26...♘d3! 27.cxd3 ♘xg2 28.♕f1 ♗xf2 29.♕xf2. I calculated up until here and thought my knight was trapped. In hindsight, it was not difficult to see 29...♘e3, but I can

safely blame my emotions for missing this chance.

27.♖xg2

At this point, I felt worried about my king. I did not want to give my opponent any counterplay with g6/♕h4.

27...f4

Better was 27...♘f3! 28.♕c3 (28.♕g3 ♖e3) 28...♖xa5!! 29.♘xa5 (29.♖xa5 ♖e1+; 29.♕xa5 f4!!) 29...♖e3, beautifully trapping the queen in the middle of the board.

28.♕c3

28...♘c4

Threatening ...♖e3 or ...♘e3 with ...♕xh3+ to follow.

Initially when I played 27...f4, I had planned 28...f3 as the next move, but I could not find anything after 29.♖h2. I did not notice 29...♖xa5!!, followed by ...f2, winning for Black.

29.♕f3 ♕f5

At this point we were both getting low on time, although I always had 10 minutes more than Irina.

30.♘xc5?!

Instead, 30.g6! would have yielded unpleasant counterplay.

30...♕xc5 31.b4 ♕f5

Here I felt confident again. My

king was much safer than hers, the f4-pawn had given me an obvious advantage, and my knight was much better than her bishop on a5. I just had to keep my advantage and make the time-control. And of course, I had to stay calm and not let my emotions get the better of me.

32.♖f2 ♖e4 33.♖g1 ♖ae8

34.♗c7??

A blunder that was caused by a lot of positional and time-pressure.
She should have gone 34.♔h2 ♖e3 35.♕g4 ♕e5, when Black is still much better but not close to winning yet.

34...♖e3

I had seen this move before, but I took my time here to triple-check and make sure I was actually winning the queen.

35.♕xf4 ♖xh3+ 36.♔g2 ♘e3+
37.♕xe3 ♕g4+ 38.♕g3 ♖xg3+
39.♗xg3 ♖e3 40.♔h2 ♕h5+

I did it! I won the queen and made the time-control. I left the board for a couple of minutes, got a snack, drank some tea, and pulled myself together one last time to finish the game strongly.

41.♔g2 ♕xg5 42.♔h2 ♖e6

America's got talent. In her debut 12-year-old Carissa Yip defeated seven-time champion Irina Krush.

43.♖gg2 ♕h5+ 44.♔g1 ♕d1+
45.♖f1 ♕d4+ 46.♖ff2 ♖e1+
47.♔h2 ♕d1 48.♗f4 ♕h5+
49.♔g3 ♖h1 50.♗h2 ♖g1+
51.♖hg2 ♖h1 52.♖h2 ♕g6+
53.♔h3 ♕e6+ 54.♔g3 ♖e1

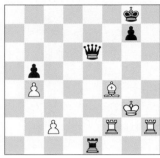

I made some unnecessary moves, but she was the one who needed to be careful. I had full control of the position and I was not in a hurry to win. My only job was to not blunder any pieces, as the position was completely winning.

55.♖hg2 ♕g6+ 56.♔h2 ♕e4
57.♗g5 ♕xb4 58.♗f4 ♕e7
59.♔g3 ♖e6 60.♔h3 ♕d7
61.♔h2 ♖e4 62.♔g3 ♕f5 63.♖f3
g5!

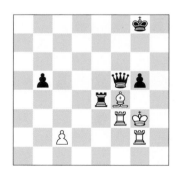

And ...g5 again, my final tactic.
64.♗xg5 White is also lost after 64.♗d2 ♖g4+ 65.♔f2 ♖xg2+ 66.♔xg2 ♕xc2 67.♖f2 b4.
64...♖g4+
She resigned and congratulated me. Words cannot describe the relief and happiness I felt in that very moment. I consider becoming the 2016 US Women's Champion the biggest accomplishment so far in my career. ∎

MAXIMize your Tactics

with Maxim Notkin

Find the best move in the positions below

Solutions on page 105

1. Black to move

2. White to move

3. White to move

4. Black to move

5. Black to move

6. Black to move

7. White to move

8. Black to move

9. White to move

SECRETS OF OPENING SURPRISES

A severe case of 'prophylactitis' against the Najdorf

JEROEN BOSCH

6.♘b3!?

'Bartel managed an astounding 4 out of 5, and an Elo performance of well over 2900!'

The perennial problem of all 1.e4 players is: what to play against the Najdorf? You can opt for one of the main lines – learning loads of theory by heart – and end up with no opening advantage. Or you can pick one of the sub-lines, and end up with no opening advantage. The choice is yours!

In the months of March and April of this year, Mateusz Bartel made his choice. In five games the Polish grandmaster played 6.♘b3 against a Najdorf-squad with an average rating of nearly 2700 (Gelfand, Wojtaszek, Ragger, Artemiev and Swiercz). His score, you are wondering? He managed an astounding 4 out of 5, and an Elo performance of well over 2900! At first sight, withdrawing the knight from d4 without sufficient provocation seems like a bad case of 'prophylacti-tis'. Indeed, the disease's most prominent victim was the 9th World Champion Tigran Petrosian, of whom it was said that he could detect and prevent his opponents' threats well before they had even entered their minds.

Personally, I was not too surprised by 6.♘b3, and not because I suffer from the same disease, but because I was familiar with an article by Dutch GM Dimitri Reinderman in SOS-14 (New In Chess, 2012). In this article, Reinderman explains how he came into contact with a Swedish amateur called Jacob Mejvik, who had enthusiastically sent him his analysis of 6.♘b3, part of which he had

done together with Swedish GM Nils Grandelius. Bartel's recent games certainly shed new, and bright, light on the matter.

1.e4 c5 2.♘f3 d6 3.d4 cxd4 4.♘xd4 ♘f6 5.♘c3 a6 6.♘b3!?
Such a 'laissez-faire' approach will give your opponent a lot of leeway of course. To my mind, the most serious options for Black now are: 6...♘c6, 6...g6, 6...e6 and 6...♘bd7. These will be our main lines, and we will use Bartel's games as our guideline. However, let's discuss a few other 'typical Najdorf' moves first.
■ 6...e5?! seems a tad silly here. Why give White the option to transpose to a traditional line of his liking (7.♗e2, 7.♗e3, 7.a4, 7.g3) and give him some extra options as well? That's certainly no way to refute 6.♘b3.
7.♗g5 is the most logical option perhaps, since 6.♗g5 is never met by 6...e5.

■ Not worthy of a serious discussion is 6...♕c7?!, when Reinderman gives 7.♘d5!? as an interesting option (which it certainly is), while 7.♗g5 and 7.♗e3 are both fine too.

■ 6...b5 is another Najdorf move, but I think it is early days for this advance here.

7.♗d3 was played by GM Zapata, but I wouldn't recommend it especially. White has two interesting alternatives:

– 7.e5 dxe5 8.♕f3 ♖a7 9.♗e3 is sharp and will yield considerable compensation for the pawn. This is a line that Mejvik has analysed, and Reinderman endorses it with further analysis in SOS-14 to a point where he thinks that it leads to equal chances.

– Personally, I like the positional 7.a4 b4 8.♘d5, and here 8...♘xe4? fails to 9.♕f3! f5 10.♗d3, and White is better.

Variation I
Bartel-Gelfand
Moscow 2016

6...♘c6 The next few moves are logical enough to have occurred several times in practice.
7.♗e3 e6 8.g4 b5 9.♗g2 ♗b7 10.g5 ♘d7 11.f4

11...♘b6
Here the lines diverged.
– 11...b4 12.♘a4 ♘a5 13.♘d2 ♖c8, and now, rather than 14.a3?! bxa3 15.b3?! (15.♖xa3) 15...♗e7 16.0-0 0-0 17.h4 (17.♖xa3 e5!) 17...d5, Valuet-Petkov, Juvisy-sur-Orge 2013, White should go 14.0-0! ♗e7 15.c3 bxc3 16.♘xc3 0-0 17.♕h5 to play for an attack.
– 11...♗e7 12.♕g4 (12.0-0!? h6 13.g6 is unclear, according to Gofshtein) 12...♘a5 13.♘xa5 ♕xa5 14.0-0 0-0 15.a3, with a typical Sicilian middlegame in which White seems to be slightly better; Betko-Mirumian, Olomouc 1998.
12.♕e2!
Bartel is prepared to give up his dark-squared bishop for Black's knight. He prepares castling queenside to start playing against Black's uncastled king.
12...♘c4 13.0-0-0 ♘xe3
The knight made five moves to 'win' a bishop that had moved only once. Consequently, White has a clear edge in development.
14.♕xe3 ♘a5 Or 14...♗e7, when 15.h4! prepares f4-f5. The sharp 14...b4 can be met by 15.♘a4, but also by the piece sacrifice 15.♘d5!? exd5 16.exd5+ ♘e7 17.f5.
15.f5
The engines also like 15.♕h3, which comes with the positional threat of g5-g6.
15...♘c4 16.♕g3 b4
16...♗e7 17.h4 b4 18.fxe6!? fxe6 (18...bxc3 19.exf7+ ♔xf7 20.♕xc3) 19.♘e2, and pawn e6 is weak.

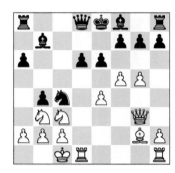

17.♘a4 17.♘e2 is met by 17...e5. However, 17.e5 leads to fantastic complications that may favour White.

For example: 17...♗xg2 18.♕xg2 ♘xe5 19.♖he1! bxc3 20.♖xe5 ♗e7 21.♕c6+ ♔f8 22.fxe6 ♗g5+ 23.♔b1.
17...e5 18.♘ac5 ♗c6 19.♗f1! ♘b6 20.♘xa6 ♗e7 21.f6 gxf6 **22.♘xb4** 22.gxf6! ♗xf6 23.♗f3 and White is better. **22...♗xe4 23.♗g2** 23.♗b5+! ♔f8 24.gxf6 ♗xf6 25.♖hg1. **23...♗g6** 23...♗xg2 24.♕xg2 f5. **24.♗xa8** 24.♗c6+! ♔f8 25.♗xa8 ♕xa8 26.gxf6 ♗xf6 27.♕f2. **24...♕xa8 25.♕f2 ♘d7 26.♘d5 ♕xa2 27.gxf6 ♗f8 28.♕d2?** This is a blunder that goes unpunished. Correct was 28.♕e3 h5 29.♘b4. **28...h5?** 28...♘c5! wins. **29.♘c3** 29.♘b4. **29...♕a6 30.♕f2 ♗h6+ 31.♔b1 0-0** White is still up for preference, but after many more complications the game ended in a draw on move 77.

Variation II
Bartel-Artemiev
Moscow 2016

6...g6
The Dragon is another logical option.
7.♗e2
7.e5!? isn't totally stupid, according to Reinderman in SOS-14. Indeed, 7...dxe5 8.♕xd8+ ♔xd8 9.♗g5 ♗g7 10.0-0-0+ certainly yields very decent compensation for the pawn.

This could be a good starting position for your own research!
7...♗g7 8.g4
8.0-0 may lead to the Classical line against the Dragon. Black is already committed to ...a6 (which is not so bad), but he retains the option of moving the queen's knight to d7 rather than to c6.

$\unicode{x2658}$c6 10.$\unicode{x2655}$d2 transposes to a game Kim-Tologontegin, Voronezh 2006 , while 9...$\unicode{x2657}$xg5!? 10.$\unicode{x2657}$xg5 $\unicode{x2655}$xg5 11.$\unicode{x2655}$xd6 is a slight edge for White.

– 8.$\unicode{x2657}$g2 $\unicode{x2658}$c6 9.f4 g5!? 10.e5! dxe5 11.$\unicode{x2655}$xd8+ $\unicode{x2654}$xd8 12.fxg5 $\unicode{x2658}$d5 13.$\unicode{x2658}$xd5 exd5 14.$\unicode{x2657}$xd5 $\unicode{x2657}$xg4 15.$\unicode{x2657}$e3, with a tiny edge in V.Onischuk-Atabayev, Kazan 2013.

8.$\unicode{x2657}$g2 $\unicode{x2657}$b7 9.g5 b4!? Or 9...$\unicode{x2658}$fd7.
10.$\unicode{x2658}$d5!?

10...$\unicode{x2658}$xd5?! 10...exd5 11.gxf6 dxe4 (not 11...$\unicode{x2655}$xf6 12.$\unicode{x2658}$a5!) is very unclear. White has a 'free' move now, for 12...$\unicode{x2655}$xf6 is not a threat due to 13.$\unicode{x2658}$a5. So moves like 12.$\unicode{x2655}$g4, 12.$\unicode{x2655}$h5 and 12.$\unicode{x2657}$e3 all come into consideration.
11.exd5 e5 12.a3!
White has emerged from the opening with a positional edge, which is not bad against a Najdorf expert like Wojtaszek!
12...$\unicode{x2657}$e7 White is better after 12...bxa3 13.$\unicode{x2656}$xa3 a5 (13...$\unicode{x2657}$e7 14.$\unicode{x2658}$a5!) 14.$\unicode{x2655}$e2!?, planning 14...a4 15.$\unicode{x2658}$d4.
13.axb4! $\unicode{x2657}$xg5 14.$\unicode{x2658}$a5 $\unicode{x2657}$c8

Now best would have been 15.c4!, but **15.$\unicode{x2657}$xg5?! $\unicode{x2655}$xg5 16.$\unicode{x2655}$f3 0-0 17.$\unicode{x2655}$g3** was also pleasant for White, although slightly less clear. Bartel won on move 58.

8...h6?!
I don't like this move at all. Bartel now just opts for the typical Rauzer attack against the Dragon. Admittedly, White has voluntarily moved his knight away from the centre, but ...a6 and ...h6 aren't great contributions to Black's cause. In fact, ...h6 is a serious weakness forcing Black's king to stay in the centre.
Let's look at a 'normal' Dragon: 8...$\unicode{x2658}$c6 9.$\unicode{x2657}$e3 $\unicode{x2657}$e6 10.g5 (10.f4 0-0?! would actually transpose to a dangerous line in the Dragon called the Rabinovich Attack – in which Black has played an inferior move – 10...a6. Castling on move 10 is therefore a mistake, but this doesn't mean that 10.f4 is totally stupid) 10...$\unicode{x2658}$d7 11.$\unicode{x2655}$d2 $\unicode{x2656}$c8 12.0-0-0 $\unicode{x2658}$a5 13.$\unicode{x2658}$d5 (13.$\unicode{x2657}$d4! gives White a plus) 13...$\unicode{x2658}$xb3+?! (13...$\unicode{x2658}$c4 14.$\unicode{x2657}$xc4 $\unicode{x2656}$xc4 15.f3 is a typically complex Dragon, in which I think Black ought to be fine) 14.axb3 $\unicode{x2658}$c5 (this double attack was Black's point) 15.$\unicode{x2654}$b1! $\unicode{x2658}$xe4 16.$\unicode{x2655}$b4 $\unicode{x2658}$c5 17.h4! 0-0 18.h5 $\unicode{x2657}$f5 19.hxg6 fxg6 (19...hxg6 20.$\unicode{x2655}$h4 $\unicode{x2656}$e8 21.$\unicode{x2657}$g4!; 19...$\unicode{x2657}$xg6 20.$\unicode{x2655}$h4 $\unicode{x2656}$e8 21.$\unicode{x2657}$h5) 20.$\unicode{x2657}$c4? (20.$\unicode{x2655}$h4! $\unicode{x2658}$xb3 21.$\unicode{x2657}$c4! $\unicode{x2656}$xc4 22.$\unicode{x2655}$xc4, winning) 20... e6 21.$\unicode{x2657}$xc5 $\unicode{x2656}$xc5 22.$\unicode{x2658}$e3 Horvath-Schachinger, Austria tt-2 2015/16, and now 22...$\unicode{x2655}$xg5 23.$\unicode{x2658}$xf5 $\unicode{x2655}$xf5 would have favoured Black.
9.$\unicode{x2657}$e3 $\unicode{x2658}$c6 10.f3 b5 10...0-0 11.$\unicode{x2655}$d2 $\unicode{x2654}$h7 12.h4 is decidedly awkward for Black. **11.$\unicode{x2655}$d2 $\unicode{x2657}$e6 12.0-0-0 $\unicode{x2656}$c8 13.$\unicode{x2654}$b1 $\unicode{x2658}$e5**
True, Black's pieces harmonize beautifully on the queenside, but his own king position is a serious headache.
14.h4 $\unicode{x2658}$c4 15.$\unicode{x2657}$d4!

15...$\unicode{x2655}$c7 15...$\unicode{x2658}$c6 16.g5! $\unicode{x2658}$xd4 17.gxf6 is the tactical justification of 15.$\unicode{x2657}$d4: 17...$\unicode{x2658}$xe2 18.fxg7 $\unicode{x2658}$xc3+ 19.$\unicode{x2655}$xc3 $\unicode{x2656}$g8 20.$\unicode{x2655}$e3 and White is better.
16.f4 $\unicode{x2657}$xe2? After 16...$\unicode{x2658}$c6 17.$\unicode{x2657}$xf6! $\unicode{x2657}$xf6 18.$\unicode{x2658}$d5 $\unicode{x2657}$xd5 19.exd5 $\unicode{x2658}$b8 20.g5 White is better.
17.$\unicode{x2655}$xe2 $\unicode{x2658}$exg4 17...$\unicode{x2658}$c4 18.e5 is no better. **18.e5** White just crashes through now. **18...dxe5 19.fxe5** Black loses a piece. **19...$\unicode{x2655}$c4 20.exf6** 20.$\unicode{x2656}$d3 0-0 21.exf6 $\unicode{x2658}$xf6 22.$\unicode{x2655}$xe7 was even more precise. **20...$\unicode{x2655}$xe2 21.$\unicode{x2658}$xe2 $\unicode{x2657}$xf6 22.h5 g5 23.$\unicode{x2658}$g3 $\unicode{x2657}$xd4 24.$\unicode{x2656}$xd4** Some technique is still required now, as Black has two pawns for a knight, but Bartel managed quite adequately.

Variation III
Bartel-Wojtaszek
Poznan 2016
6...e6 This is certainly sound, and Wojtaszek played this 'Scheveningen' move the first time he was confronted with 6.$\unicode{x2658}$b3.
7.g4 Bartel always likes this thrust on the kingside.

7...b5 In case of the natural 7...$\unicode{x2657}$e7 there are two options:
– It's possible to play 8.g5 $\unicode{x2658}$fd7, as 9.$\unicode{x2657}$e3

Variation IV
Bartel-Ragger
Germany Bundesliga 2015/16

6...♘bd7

Both Ragger and Swiercz developed their queen's knight to this square, and that in games only days apart!

7.g4

This is Bartel's preferred way of playing against the Najdorf. He embarks on a kind of 'Keres Attack'.

Actually, 7.♗e3 is a very serious move here, since 7...e5?! 8.f3! leads to a position from the 6.♗e3 Najdorf that favours White: 6.♗e3 e5 7.♘b3, and now Black plays 7...♗e6 or 7...♗e7 and not 7...♘bd7?! 8.f3, which leads to our present position. An example is Tiviakov-Gelfand, Elista 1998: 8...b5?! 9.a4! b4 10.♘d5 ♘xd5 11.♕xd5 ♖b8 12.♗c4 ♕f6 13.♘a5 and White is better.

7...h6 8.a4

This Bundesliga game was played only two days after Bartel had last played his pet line in the 9th round of the Polish Championship.

In that game, Bartel had opted for 8.♗g2 b5 9.h4 b4 10.♘d5 ♘xd5 11.exd5 ♘e5.

This pretty weird position is probably quite OK for Black. Bartel now deviated from Kanarek-Wojtaszek, Poznan 2016, a game that had been played one day earlier and had ended in a convincing victory for Wojtaszek: 12.g5!? (after 12.f3?! g6! 13.♗e3 ♗g7 14.♗d4 0-0 Black has a simple plan in the form of ...a5-a4, while there is disharmony in White's camp, Kanarek-Wojtaszek, Poznan 2016 (8)) 12...hxg5 13.♗xg5 ♗g4 (here, too, a case can be made for 13...a5!?) 14.f3 (14.♕d2 ♗f3!) 14...♗h5 15.♕e2 ♕c7 16.0-0-0.

Compared to Kanarek-Wojtaszek, White is much better off here. He has managed to castle, and despite the oddly disjointed pawns on h4, f3 and d5, he has a few trumps: a safe king and an edge in development, for example. The position offers chances to both sides. 16...g6 17.♘d4 ♗g7 18.♗h3!?, eyeing the c8-square and preparing ♗h3-g4. 18...♖b8 19.♔b1 a5 20.♗g4 ♕c4! (Swiercz exchanges queens before things get too hot for his king) 21.♕xc4 ♘xc4 22.♘c6 ♖b7 23.♖de1 ♗xg4 24.fxg4 ♘e5, with equal chances, Bartel-Swiercz, Poznan 2016 (9).

The text-move (8.a4) is a much more positional approach, aimed at castling kingside.

8...♕c7 9.♗g2 ♘e5 10.h3 g5

This is actually a fairly common concept in the Najdorf for Black – take for example the line 6.h3 e6 7.g4 h6 8.♗g2 g5!?. Black controls as many dark squares as possible, and if White were to play f2-f4, Black would have at least an invulnerable knight on e5 (after ...gxf4).

11.f4 gxf4 12.♗xf4 ♗g7

12...♘c4 probably forces 13.♗c1, but after 13...♗g7 14.0-0 it is very likely that the knight will have to return to e5 anyway to keep Black's position together.

13.♕e2 ♗d7 14.0-0!?

There are alternatives, but in any case the middlegame is very tense and offers chances to both sides.

14...♖c8 15.♖f2

Bartel opts for a clear plan: doubling on the f-file and concentrating all his forces on the kingside and in the centre.

15...♕c4 16.♕d2 ♕c7 17.♖af1 ♘c4 18.♕e2 ♗e6 Ragger's intention must have been 18...♘xb2, but he was rightly scared of the complications after 19.e5! ♕xc3, and now 20.exd6!?, which seems difficult to defend for Black.

19.♘d5 ♘xd5 20.exd5 ♗d7 21.c3

At this point it seems that Black's concept has failed. His king has remained in the centre and is now facing the storm. Black's only trump is the e5-square.

21...♗e5 22.♗c1! f6 23.♘d4 ♘b6?! 24.♕e4

The storm is gathering. White is superior and Bartel won on move 38.

Conclusion

I hope that by now you are convinced that 6.♘b3 is more than a bad case of 'prophylactitis'. Instead of preventing his opponent's options Bartel has, in fact, very aggressive intentions with the knight retreat, aiming as he does for the g4-thrust. Let's all follow suit! ■

Back to the future

Kasparov steals the show in Ultimate Blitz Challenge

He was not the favourite and he didn't win, but all eyes were on Garry Kasparov at the Ultimate Blitz Challenge in St. Louis. And rightly so. **ANISH GIRI** thoroughly enjoyed the show and happily pays tribute to his childhood hero. The great man himself makes the fun complete by annotating one of his finest efforts.

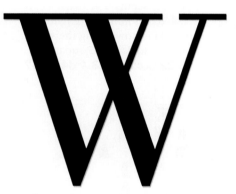

When I first heard that there was going to be a special chess event in St. Louis (where else!) featuring Garry Kasparov, I was mildly excited. As a chess fan and a Kasparov fan (but isn't that the same thing?) I was obviously quite happy to see my childhood hero back at the chessboard again. However, knowing how strict Kasparov used to be about his retirement, I assumed that the event would one way or another feature some strange form of chess or some unusual participants, or, God forbid, Nigel Short. Nope, this time around it was different altogether. The Ulti-mate Blitz Challenge with Garry Kasparov turned out to be a serious blitz tournament with 18(!!) rounds played between the top-three finish-ers of the 2016 US Chess champion-ships (presumably Fabiano Caruana, Hikaru Nakamura and Wesley So) and the old Boss, Garry Kasparov.

A daring challenge for the chess legend, considering that all three top Americans are in the world's Top 10. On the other hand, Garry Kimovich really has little to lose or to prove, so his participation was less shocking than it may have seemed at first sight.

And so, after I had mentally put this event on the list of things I was looking forward to, I went on with my life. That is, until I lost a couple of games in Norway Chess, Fabiano confessed his undying love for Law-rence Trent in the St. Louis confes-sion box, and that same Fabiano won the US Championship. Now it was

Some things never change. When Garry Kasparov sits down to play chess, excited fans around the world tune in to see the Boss in action.

high time for the grand dessert of the US Championships, in other words for Hashtag Ultimate Blitz at the Saint Louis Chess Club and Scholastic Center.

I thoroughly enjoyed the event and hope I will manage to convey my enthusiasm, even though I am not much of a story teller. But I do like chess, so perhaps instead of trying to squeeze words out of myself, let me try to tell this story through the games of Garry Kasparov. And I do hope that the winner of the event, Hikaru Nakamura, will forgive me for focussing on the number 3 finisher. At the end of the day, Garry Kasparov playing chess these days is far, far rarer than Hikaru Nakamura winning tournaments. And, critical reader, I would like you to forgive me, too, since there may be some exaggeration and sheer worship in the following notes, even if it's only Kasparov making decent

moves. But hey, you must have seen my critical side far too often to be missing it already.

This is what happened when Kasparov sat down for his first game.

SO 4.4 – C45
Garry Kasparov
Wesley So
St. Louis blitz 2016 (1)

The first game is always important, as it gives you an idea of where you stand. I am sure that Garry Kimovich, after quite some years of not facing the best players in the world, wanted to find out where he stood.
1.e4 e5 2.♘f3 ♘c6 3.d4
I smiled here, and I'm sure many of my colleagues did, too. I'm not sure about So, but that can be traced back thanks to the excellent video coverage by Team Randy (Randy Sinquefield owns the TV company that

broadcasts the events at the Saint Louis Chess Club – ed.). The Scotch has been Kasparov's way of avoiding the Berlin even before the Berlin really existed.
3...exd4 4.♘xd4

4...♘f6
4...♗c5 appeared in many of Kasparov's games later on in the tournament.
5.♘xc6 bxc6 6.e5 ♕e7 7.♕e2 ♘d5 8.c4 ♗a6 9.b3

♘d2, here and even on the previous move, has been the trend recently, but I am not going to doubt the fact that Garry did his homework for this event and neither should you.

9...g6 10. ♗a3!?

A novelty by Kasparov, played by him in 1994... only a month before I was born.

10...c5?!

Wesley lashed out some normal move, but the price of a move in this opening is quite high and from here on in he is forced onto the defensive.

10...♘b4 was played in a high-level game four years ago, while I was sitting at the board next to it: 11.♗b2 ♗g7 12.a3 ♘d5 13.♘d2 0-0 14.0-0-0, when a sharp game ensued and Peter Leko eventually outclassed his opponent: Landa-Leko, Sochi 2012, 0-1.

10...♕g5 was the first game in this variation. Quite curiously, after 11.g3 ♘c3 12.♘xc3 ♗xa3 13.♘e4 ♕e7 14.♘f6+ ♔f8 15.♗g2 ♗b4+ 16.♔f1 both kings lost the right to castle, and before they could do so artificially, a move repetition took place: 16...♖d8 17.♕b2 ♗a3 18.♕c3 ♗b4 19.♕b2 ♗a3 20.♕c3 ♗b4 ½-½, Kasparov-Ivanchuk, Amsterdam 1994.

11.g3 ♗g7 12.f4 ♘b4 13. ♗g2 ♖d8 14. ♘c3 0-0

It feels as if the opening has really gone wrong for So. Here Kasparov plays a very forcing move, consolidating his plus, although it's quite possible that the simple 15.0-0 or even 15.0-0-0!? would have been stronger.

15. ♗b2!?

For a second I was puzzled, but obviously the threat is a3.

15...d5! 16.a3! d4 17.axb4 dxc3 18. ♗xc3 cxb4 19. ♗b2?!

This move is aimed against ...f6, which worked out excellently in the game, but objectively speaking the alternative was stronger:

19.♗d2!. Going for the a7-pawn and keeping the option of solidifying the g1-a7 diagonal with ♗e3!. Now 19...♗c8 20.0-0 f6 21.♖a4 c5 22.♗d5+ would force Black to give up an exchange, just as he did in the game.

19... ♗c8!

The bishop is finally back in business. Here, to be honest, I started liking Black's position, but before I started worrying for my childhood hero, Wesley managed to get a lost position.

20.0-0

20...f6? This is just a blunder. 20...♗f5 would be highly unpleasant to meet. For now ...♗d3 is a threat: 21.♖fd1 (21.♕f2 is met solidly by 21...♖d3, with some real counterplay) 21...♖xd1+ 22.♖xd1 ♖d8, and Black is totally fine here.

21. ♗d5+! And since 21...♔h8 falls for a very neat tactic, Black is forced to give up an exchange for no compensation. The rest was a matter of converting, which is never easy in a blitz game, but here White is just much too in control.

21...♖xd5 As 21...♔h8 runs into 22.exf6! (ouch!) 22...♕xe2 (22...♕c5+ avoids the mate, but the result will be the same, even after the simple 23.♕f2) 23.fxg7 mate. **22.cxd5 ♕c5+ 23.♖f2 fxe5 24.♗xe5** From here on in, it was nice to see the steady hand of the maestro. Unfortunately, the race against time can't be won and in some of the rounds that followed, the same steady hand was sometimes missing. **24...♗xe5 25.♕xe5** And not 25.fxe5? ♗b7!. **25...♖d8 26.♖d1 ♗g4 27.♕d4! ♕a5 28.♖dd2 ♖e8 29.♔g2 ♕b5 30.h3 ♗f5 31.g4 ♗e4+ 32.♔h2 c5 33.♕f6 c4 34.d6 ♗c6 35.f5 ♖f8 36.♕e6+ ♔g7 37.d7 ♕c5 38.♕d6** Black resigned.

After this swift start an incident happened in the second round.

Nakamura-Kasparov
St. Louis blitz 2016 (2)
position after 26.fxe4

This is quite obviously a King's Indian gone wrong for Black. Still, Kasparov somehow managed to stay alive and the drawing chances seemed better than ever until 26...♞b4?? ... was sort of played, but

then it was taken back?! And replaced by: **26...♞f4!** and Black managed to draw. After 26...♞b4 27.♗c5 ♖b8 (27...♞d3 28.♗xf8 ♞xc1 29.♗xg7+! check!) 28.♗xb4 ♖xb4 29.♖c8+ it would have been game over.

The one and only Yasser Seirawan started defending the Great Champion for a while, but he himself probably didn't entirely believe the rule that you can take your move back in blitz after you let the piece go but before you press your clock, either. One way or another, Hikaru decided not to press charges. Unfortunately, this was not the last time Garry Kimovich would blunder his knight and it would remain the only time that he got away with it.

In Kasparov's third game nothing out of the ordinary happened until a study was created by accident. With only seconds left, Kasparov failed to solve it.

Kasparov-Caruana
St. Louis blitz 2016 (3)
position after 42...♞c5

Here Fabiano allowed a brilliant geometry that no player would see in a blitz game in a million years.
43.♕f6+? 43.♕e5!! ...

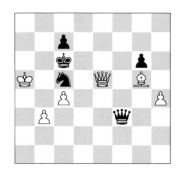

ANALYSIS DIAGRAM

... and it transpires that somehow Black is lost. A miracle.
43...♕xf6 44.♗xf6 ♞xb3+ 45.♔b4 Draw.

The following encounter undoubtedly left the legend satisfied with himself.

SO 5.6 – C45
Garry Kasparov
Hikaru Nakamura
St. Louis blitz 2016 (5)

1.e4 e5 2.♞f3 ♞c6 3.d4 The Scotch again! **3...exd4 4.♞xd4 ♗c5 5.♗e3** Traditionally the main line, which seemed exhausted. But perhaps not for blitz with ignorant kids like Hikaru and Fabiano (not that I am sure that I would fare much better). 5.♞b3 was quite trendy, with possibly some old Kasparov notes after the game Carlsen-Bacrot from Nanjing 2010.
5...♞f6 6.c3 ♞ge7 7.♗c4 ♞e5 8.♗b3!?

Not exactly new, but traditionally the main move has been the automatic 8.♗e2.
8...d6?! Not so much the move, but the approach Black is going for here is dubious. Strategically speaking, White is enjoying some plus thanks to his space advantage and potentially harmonious development. Black has to keep up the momentum, and Hikaru's next few moves don't fit this strategy.
9.0-0 0-0 9...♞g4 is pointless, something which is nicely highlighted by 10.h3!, when the f7-pawn turns out to be weak.
10.f3

10...♘7c6 11.♔h1 ♗b6 12.♘a3
A reasonable way to develop the pieces. Later on the knight will find itself slightly out of play, but at this point this is hard to foresee.
12...♔h8 13.♕d2 ♘a5

14.♘db5 Trading some pieces, while at the same time touching the c7-pawn. **14...♗xe3 15.♕xe3 ♕e7 16.♗c2?!** The pawn on a7 was hanging! He could have played 16.♘xa7!.
16...a6 17.♘d4 c5!? 18.♘e2

18...♘ac4? Kids, you don't trade knights on the rim. Hikaru surely understands that, but in blitz chess instincts take over and active piece-play and one-move threats are paramount. In this game, however,

Kasparov was able to prove that blitz chess and real chess are essentially the same kind of board games.
18...b5!, keeping the tension, would give Black fine play. White can pretend that he doesn't care about the knight on a3, but sooner or later it will start to get annoying.
19.♘xc4 ♘xc4

20.♕c1 White pulls back before moving forward, a famous technique brilliantly used by Karpov. One famous example of this is Karpov-Kasparov, Game 27 from the 1984 match (look it up, you lazy folks!). The rest of the game is exemplary.
20...f5 21.b3 ♘b6 The knight guards the d5-square, but in the long run it is absolutely awfully placed here.
22.c4! fxe4 23.♗xe4 ♗f5 24.♘g3 ♗xe4 25.♘xe4 ♖ad8 26.♖e1 ♖fe8 Now Black's only chance of freeing himself is ...d6-d5. A prophylactic move is required, but the speed with which the next move followed deserves some admiration, considering its counter-intuitive nature.

27.♕d2! As if asking for ...d5, but in fact stopping it!

27...♕f8 27...d5 28.♘c3!, and see for yourself. Black loses the pawn without any compensation.
28.♘g5 ♕f6 29.♖xe8+
The easiest. The difference between the knights becomes evident once all the pieces have been traded.
29...♖xe8 30.♖e1 ♖xe1+ 31.♕xe1 ♘d7 32.♕e8+ ♘f8

33.h3! Here h4 was screaming to be played, but that would be naive. There is no need to give Black any targets on the kingside. When this excellent move was played a tempo, a frisson of approval went through our room.
33...♔g8 34.♘e4 ♕f4 35.♕e7
The d6-pawn will fall and the illusion of perpetual check is indeed merely an illusion.
35...♕c1+ 36.♔h2 ♕f4+ 37.♔g1 ♕c1+ 38.♔f2 ♕b2+ 39.♔g3 h5 40.♘xd6 h4+ 41.♕xh4 ♘g6 42.♕e4

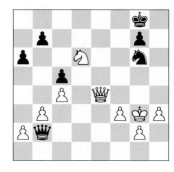

White has picked up two pawns and is still in control. The rest went smoothly as well.
42...♕f6 43.♘f5 ♕g5+ 44.♔h2 ♘f4 45.g3 ♘h5 46.f4 ♕d8 47.♕d5+ ♕xd5 48.♘e7+ ♔f7 49.♘xd5 Black resigned.

It wasn't all moonlight and roses for Kasparov, as knight blunders became a recurring theme, too. As he confessed later on in an interview, they literally led to knightmares!

So-Kasparov
St. Louis blitz 2016 (4)
position after 25.♖fd1

25...♘c3?? 26.♖c1 Yuck. 1-0.

Kasparov-So
St. Louis blitz 2016 (7)
position after 39...♖a6

A great game by Kasparov so far, but:
40.♖b1 ♖b8 41.b7?? ♕xd6 0-1.

Nakamura-Kasparov
St. Louis blitz 2016 (8)
position after 43.♘xd8

So far the game had been insane,

but the following move is a rare blunder – not entirely obvious, but it can be refuted in three ways!
43...♖d5??
This looked very clever at first (43...♔xd8 was just a draw, with Black being the one trying to utilize his chances thanks to White's poor king in the corner). Curiously enough, all sensible moves by the d8-knight win here, since the remaining knight will fork via either e5 or c5.
44.♘xf7 The rest is agony. **44...♘g4 45.♘fe5+ ♘xe5 46.♘xe5+ ♔d6 47.♖c6+ ♔e7 48.♔g1 b3 49.♖b6 ♖d1+ 50.♔f2 ♖d2+ 51.♔f3 ♖xh2 52.♘xg6+** 1-0.

Without the knight blunders, Garry Kimovich wasn't completely invulnerable either, as witness the following game.

KF 9.7 – A41
Wesley So
Garry Kasparov
St. Louis blitz 2016 (10)
1.♘f3 g6 2.e4 ♗g7 3.d4 d6 4.c4 ♗g4
I have no idea why he went for this opening, but seriously, choosing the right opening has been one of Kasparov's strongest points throughout his career.
5.♗e2 ♘c6 6.♘bd2

Not the usual way of playing, but it looks quite interesting. The pawn on d4 can't be taken. See for yourself.
6...e5 7.d5 ♘ce7 8.h3 ♗d7 9.c5!?
Now the knight on d2 finds itself quite well placed .

9...dxc5 10.♘c4 f6 11.d6 ♘c8 12.♗e3

12.b6? Too academic; more radical measures were needed: 12...b5!.
13.0-0 ♗c6
This allows a beautiful follow-up.
14.dxc7 ♕xc7 15.b4! Sweet!

15...cxb4 Again, 15...b5! was called for, better late than never, when an immediate fiasco could have been avoided.
16.♖c1 The rest is just a beautiful demonstration of why people keep talking about piece development and king safety.
16...♘ge7 17.♕b3

Castling has been stopped forever. Black's position is beyond recovery.
17...h6 18.♖fd1 b5

19.♘cxe5

I would love to put an exclam after this move, but everything wins, even 19.♘a5!?.

19...fxe5 20.♗xb5 ♖b8

21.♗a4! Painful!
21...♕b7 22.♖xc6 ♘xc6
23.♕e6+ ♘8e7 24.♗c5 ♖c8
25.♗xe7 Black resigned.

As Kasparov put it, pride aside, the game looked like Morphy against Amateurs. Things happen.

And finally let's give the mike to the hero of this story. In the final round, his old friend the KID served him well, as he beat the new US champion in great style. Caruana will not have enjoyed the black pieces hovering around his king, but for us it was a game reminiscent of Kasparov's best days.

NOTES BY
Garry Kasparov

EO 64.4 – A05
Fabiano Caruana
Garry Kasparov
St. Louis blitz 2016 (18)

This game took place in the 18th and final round, and first place was already out of reach. Before the event, I joked that the order of the draw would make for acceptable final standings, with Nakamura first and me second! I suppose this illustrates that my natural optimism isn't as rusty as my chess. And considering the number of atrocious blunders I committed, finishing third, half a point behind Wesley So, was a victory of sorts. I also took consolation in winning my mini-match against the incredibly speedy Nakamura, albeit thanks in part to his courteously allowing our game to continue when I had a 'senior moment' touch move in our second-round game. Unfortunately, Caissa is a greedy goddess and in exchange for this one pardoned knight, I lost three others during the event!

With no disrespect to my distinguished peers Karpov and Short, against whom I have won exhibition matches since my retirement in 2005, St. Louis was an entirely different thing. I was facing three top-10 players and had had very little time to prepare myself for a return to the board. As I said, I'm an optimist, but I also knew there was a real chance of total disaster. I played better and with much more energy on the first day, despite scoring more points on the second. I had illusions of settling down and having a better result, but it was not to be.

Multiple blunders in winning positions took much of the joy out of the tournament for me, and I've never played my best when in a frustrated mood. In particular, scoring a half point from two winning positions against Caruana and So in Rounds 6 and 7 left me deflated. I played two of my best efforts, only to draw the first and lose the second. If you showed me the Caruana position with my pawn on f2 and the So game with my favourite 'octopus knight' on d6 and told me that I would fail to win either game, I would never believe it!

Caruana-Kasparov
St. Louis blitz 2016 (6)
position after 33...f2

Kasparov-So
St. Louis blitz 2016 (7)
position after 32.♘xd6

Had I finished off those two games, I would have been in contention to win the tournament. Not because of my score, but because I wouldn't have lost my concentration so appallingly. As Nietzsche wrote, the forgetful are blessed because they triumph even over their own blunders in the end. Unable to forget, I allowed these blunders to cost me even more dearly for the rest of the event.

St. Louis 2016 blitz		1	2	3	4	
1	Hikaru Nakamura	* * * * * *	0 1 ½ 1 1 ½	½ 0 1 ½ 1 ½ 0	1 0 1 ½ 1 1	11
2	Wesley So	1 0 ½ 0 0 ½	* * * * * *	0 1 1 1 ½ ½	0 ½ 1 1 ½ 1	10
3	Garry Kasparov	½ 1 0 ½ 0 ½ 1	1 0 0 0 ½ ½	* * * * * *	½ ½ 1 1 0 1	9½
4	Fabiano Caruana	0 1 0 ½ 0 0	1 ½ 0 0 ½ 0	½ ½ 0 0 1 0	* * * * * *	5½

1.♘f3 ♘f6 It's a cliché at this point to bring it up, but I worked on the positions that arise in this game long before Caruana was born in 1992 – in fact, when I was much younger than he is today! My investigations began after a bad experience against Nikolaevsky's double fianchetto in 1976. And then I also suffered against Jussupow in Leningrad in April 1977. After these experiences I looked for improvements and arrived at the c5-d6-e5 structure. A few years later I revisited it with greater satisfaction against Webb at the European Team Championship and against Tempone at the World Junior.

2.g3 g6

3.♗g2

3.b3 ♗g7 4.♗b2

A. 4...d6 5.d4 0-0 6.♗g2 e5 7.dxe5 ♘fd7 8.♘c3 ♘xe5 9.♘xe5 ♗xe5 ½-½ (41) Jussupow-Kasparov, Leningrad 1977.

B. 4...c5 5.c4 d6, and now:

B1. 6.d4 ♘e4!? (this is the idea I prepared with Magerramov to meet d4. He later used the queen sac against Lev Psakhis in 1978) 7.♗g2 ♕a5+ 8.♘fd2 ♘xd2 9.♗c3

ANALYSIS DIAGRAM

> ## 'Multiple blunders in winning positions took much of the joy out of the tournament for me, and I've never played my best when in a frustrated mood.'

9...♘xb3. Our original idea; of course the computer today has a different opinion. But in 1977, Jobs and Wozniak were trying to sell the Apple II and using a computer to prepare chess analysis was as much science fiction as science. (9...♕b6! is a strong machine improvement on a 29-year-old idea! 10.dxc5 ♘xb1 11.♗xg7 ♕b4+ 12.♔f1 ♖g8 13.♗h6 g5 (13...♘a3)) 10.♗xa5 ♘xa5

ANALYSIS DIAGRAM

11.♕a4+ (a bad move – after 11.♘c3! ♘bc6 12.♖c1 ♘xd4 (12...♗xd4 13.♘b5) 13.♘b5 0-0 14.♘xd4 ♗xd4 15.♕a4 ♘c6 16.e3 ♗g7 White is better, but it is not a refutation of our idea) 11...♘ac6 12.♘d2 0-0 13.♖b1 cxd4 14.0-0 ♘d7 15.♕a3 a5 16.♖b5 a4 17.♖fb1 ♘c5 18.♘b3 axb3 19.♕xa8 ♗f5 20.♕a3 ♗xb1 21.axb3 d3 22.exd3 ♘d4 23.♖xc5 dxc5 24.♗xb7 ♘xd3 25.♕xc5 ♘xb3 26.♕c7 ♘d4 27.♕xe7 ♖xc4 28.♔g2 ♔g7 29.h4 h5 30.♗e4 ♗f6 31.♕b4 ♗e6 32.♗d3 ♖d8 33.♕b5 ♘d4 34.♕b1 ♗f5 35.♗e4 ♗xe4+ 36.♕xe4

♘f5 37.♔h3 ♖d2 38.♕f4 ♖b2 39.f3 ♘d4 40.g4 ♖f2 0-1, Psakhis-Magerramov, Baku 1978.

B2. 6.♗g2 e5 7.0-0 ♘c6 8.♘c3 0-0 9.d3 ♘e8, and now:

B21. 10.♕d2 ♘c7 11.♘e1 ♗e6 12.♘d5 ♕d7 13.e3 ♖ab8 14.f4 f5 15.♖c1 ♗f7 16.♘xc7 ♕xc7 17.♘f3 ♔h8 18.♖ce1 ♗g8 ½-½, Kharitonov-Kasparov, Moscow All-Union Youth Games 1977.

B22. 10.♘d2 ♘c7 11.e3 ♗e6 12.♖c1 ♕d7 13.♘e1 ♖ad8 14.♘de4 h6 15.f4 f5 16.♘f2 exf4 17.gxf4 ♗f7 18.♕d2 g5 19.♘e2 d5 20.♗xg7 ♕xg7 21.♔h1 dxc4 22.bxc4 ♘e8 23.♕c3 ♘f6 24.d4 ♗c8 0-1 (43), Tempone-Kasparov, Dortmund 1980.

3...♗g7 4.0-0 0-0 5.c4

5.d4 d6 6.b3 c5 7.♗b2 ♘c6? (a terrible move) 8.d5 ♘a5 1-0 (47), Nikolaevsky-Kasparov, Moscow 1976.

5...d6

6.b3

After 6.d4 ♘c6 7.♘c3 the game would have transposed to two other games from my Leningrad childhood, against Kharitonov and Leonid Zaid, quite a lot of nostalgia for one game, even for me.

7...♖b8 8.h3 a6 9.e4 b5 10.cxb5 axb5 11.♖e1 e6 12.d5 b4 1-0 (43), Kharitonov-Kasparov, Leningrad 1977.

7...a6 8.d5 ♘a5 9.♘d2 c5 10.♕c2 ♖b8 11.b3 b5 12.♗b2 bxc4 13.bxc4 ♘h6 14.♘cb1 1-0 (37), Zaid-Kasparov, Leningrad 1977.

6...e5 7.♗b2 c5

Arriving at the structure I decided on as the antidote to my double-fianchetto problems back in 1977.

8.e3 ♘c6 9.♘c3 ♗f5 10.d4?!
A square too far, as the game illustrates.
10...e4!

11.♘e1
11.♘g5 happened in another memorable game, my very first with the Soviet national team, against England at the European Team Championship in 1980: 11...♖e8 12.dxc5 dxc5∓ 13.♘b5 ♖e7 14.♕xd8+ ♖xd8 15.♖ad1 ♖xd1 16.♖xd1 h6 17.♘h3

ANALYSIS DIAGRAM

(the knight rots on h3 while Black exploits its absence) 17...g5 18.♘d6 ♗g4 19.♖d2 ♘e8 20.♗xg7 ♔xg7 21.♔f1 ♘xd6 22.♖xd6 ♘b4 23.a3 ♘d3 24.♘g1 ♘c1 25.h3 ♗c8 26.♘e2

♘xb3 27.♘c3 ♗e6 28.♗xe4 ♘a5 29.♗d5 ♘xc4 30.♗xc4 ♗xc4+ 31.♔e1 ♗e6 32.e4 ♗xh3 33.f4 gxf4 34.gxf4 ♖d7 35.e5 ♖xd6 36.exd6 f6 37.♘d5 ♔f7 38.♘c7 ♗d7 0-1, Webb-Kasparov, Skara 1980.
11...♖e8 12.♘c2

12...h5!?
12...♕c8 13.♘b5 ♖d8 14.d5 ♘e7 (14...♘e5? 15.♘xd6; 14...a6!?) 15.f3 was unclear in Viviani-Romanishin, Porto San Giorgio 2015.
13.♕d2 h4?!
Premature, a typical blitz move. Now h3, followed by g4, and the worst is over for White. Correct was 13...♕d7.
14.♗a3? b6
14...♘h7!? 15.d5 ♘g5.
15.♖fd1? Surprisingly, White doesn't have time for routine moves. 15.h3! was still indicated.
15...♗g4 16.♖dc1 ♕d7

White is already in serious trouble. The black pieces are arriving on the kingside ahead of any activity White can generate in the centre or on the queenside.
17.b4 Black is much better after 17.dxc5 bxc5, but White would have compensation for the exchange after

17...dxc5 18.♕xd7 ♘xd7 19.♘xe4! ♗xa1 20.♖xa1.
17...♕f5 18.♗b2 ♖ad8 19.♘b5 ♗f3 20.d5

20...♘e5 20...♘xb4 would have won quickly, but it was the final round and I was too tired to move my eyes away from the kingside: 21.♘xb4 (21.♗xf6 ♗xf6) 21...♗xg2 22.♔xg2 h3+ 23.♔f1 ♘g4, winning.
21.♗xe5 ♖xe5 22.♘e1 hxg3 23.fxg3 ♗h6 Stronger was 23...♕h5 24.h3 ♖g5 25.♕f2 ♖f5, winning.

24.♖ab1 Black also wins after 24.♘xa7 ♕h5 25.h3 ♖g5 26.♕f2 ♖f5.
24...♔g7

To involve the final piece on the board, the rook on d8, in the attack.

You cannot criticize me for lack of single-minded purpose!

25.♖b3

Black is winning after 25.bxc5 bxc5 26.♖b3 ♛h5 27.♘xa7 ♖h8.

25...♛h5 26.h3 ♘h7

Don't forget it was a blitz game. There were many more winning moves, e.g. 26...♗g4 27.♘xa7 (27.h4 g5) 27...♗xh3 28.♗xh3 (28.♘c6 ♖g5 29.♘xd8 ♖xg3) 28...♖xh3 29.♛g2 ♗xe3+! 30.♖xe3 ♛h6 31.♖cc3 ♘g4.

27.g4

White is in insurmountable trouble, as the following lines show: 27.♘xa7 ♘g5 28.h4 ♗xg2 29.♛xg2 (29.♘c6 ♘f3+ 30.♘xf3 ♗xf3 31.♘xd8 ♛g4 32.♛f2 ♖h5 33.♔f1 ♖f5) 29...♘f3+ 30.♘xf3 exf3 31.♛f2 ♖de8 32.♖e1 ♖e4 33.♘b5 ♖xh4 34.gxh4 ♖e4. Or 27.h4 g5 28.♛f2 ♗g4 29.♗f1 gxh4 30.gxh4 ♖f5 31.♛b2+ ♘f6 32.♘g2 ♔h7.

27...♗xg4! 28.hxg4 ♛xg4

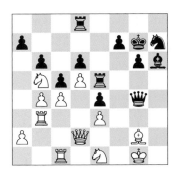

29.♛d1

29.bxc5 was more resilient, but it's not enough either: 29...♘g5 30.♘xd6 ♖xd6 31.cxd6 ♖f5 32.d7 ♛g3! 33.♛e2 (33.d8♛ ♘h3+ 34.♔h1 ♖f1+ 35.♗xf1 ♛g1 mate) 33...♘h3+

34.♔h1 ♘f2+ 35.♔g1 ♘g4 36.♛xg4 ♛xg4 37.d8♛ (37.♖c2 ♗g5) 37...♛g3!.

29...♛g3 30.♛e2 ♘g5 31.♔h1 ♖h8 32.♘xd6

32...♔g8 An amusing glitch, but luckily the position was beyond ruining even for me. I had long been planning to open up the h8-rook by moving the bishop, but it made much more sense to go forward after moving the knight than backward after moving the king.

After 32...♘f3 it's mate in 6: 33.♘xf3 ♗xe3+ 34.♔h3 ♖xh3+ 35.♘h2 ♖xh2+ 36.♛xh2 ♛f3+ 37.♛g2 ♖h5 mate.

33.bxc5 ♗f8+ 33...♘f3 leads to a quick mate here, too.

34.♔g1 ♘h3+ The most efficient was 34...♗xd6 35.cxd6 ♖f5.

35.♔f1 ♗xd6 36.cxd6 ♖f5+ 37.♘f3 ♖xf3+

It has been a rocky road, but Black finally arrives at his destination. White resigned.

I would like to thank and congratulate my young opponents for participating in this unusual challenge, and Rex Sinquefield for organizing it. These three will make up the core of a US Olympiad team that will be one of the favourites to bring home the first American gold medal since the boycotted 1976 Olympiad in Haifa.

As for me, I enjoyed the experience on the whole and will be interested to see if we can come up with another entertaining format. Next time I will try to practice a little more... ∎

In the last round Garry Kasparov defeated brand-new US Champion Fabiano Caruana with an attack that was reminiscent of his best years. Watch the black pieces hover around White's king!

At the end of the day

'Something a bit like Munch's The Scream would be a good description of how I'm coming back home after work at the moment, and I fear this may have an effect on this month's reviews', **MATTHEW SADLER** warns the reader.

Many years ago – before the start of the round at the Watson Farley Williams tournament of 1989 to be precise – I remember Patrick Wolff and other players discussing the *Informator* symbols that were actually necessary to describe the course of a game but that for some reason had never made it to the official lexicon. It started off with 'distracted by the opponent', 'needed the toilet', 'spilt coffee on my trousers' and – as you can imagine – progressed further into topics not suitable for a family magazine like this one!

I feel at the moment that similar symbols would be useful to explain how your reviewer is currently feeling. Something a bit like Munch's *The Scream* would be a good description of how I'm coming back home after work at the moment, and I fear this may have an effect on this month's reviews. In the evening, after a day of argument, chaos and confusion, I'm looking to chess for clear explanations, easy solutions, and a world of certainty and simplicity... Anything above that and I'm not taking much

in! On the one hand not great, on the other hand this is probably close to the typical amateur experience that 90% of the readers face when trying to find a bit of time for chess in between an exhausting job, sweet but demanding family members and the thousands of practical things you're supposed to sort out yourself in modern life!

■ ■ ■

This month's reviews start with a new edition of *Dynamic Chess Strategy* by Mihai Suba (New In Chess). I had completely missed the first edition in 1991 so this is my first exposure to Suba's writings. The first edition won the 1991 BCF Book of the Year award and was acclaimed as a modern classic so I was looking forward to reading it.

In the light of the introduction, let me say at once that this is not the type of book that you can read when you're tired or distracted. It's also not the type of book you can read in little bites – 15 minutes one evening, 15 minutes a couple of evenings later. This is one for during the holiday or a long quiet weekend without the children! What's the reason for this? Well, the book can be very hard to follow, and I think that you'll never really get into it if you don't understand how the book is put

together. Let me just go off on a tangent to explain my view of the book.

I remember Garry once saying that before his first match against Karpov, Botvinnik presented him solemnly with his secret analysis notebooks containing all his opening analysis from his long and distinguished career. What treasures would these notebooks hold? Garry was appalled when he read through them – how could someone become World Champion with analysis of this quality? At the time I took it to be an indication of how superior modern (well... relatively modern – he said that in 1992!) chess analysis was compared with analysis from the 1960s. However, a later experience made me wonder whether there was more to it than that.

The experience was that I started seconding Joel Lautier. At the start of our collaboration, I showed him my analyses of two openings in which I was fairly proficient: the QGA and 6.♗g5 in the KID Sämisch. It was a confusing experience. Joel confronted me continually with questions and queries. Some of them were of course completely valid, but for others I thought to myself (stressed, guilty and ashamed): 'But you can't be worried about that line? That's just easy to play – you don't need analysis for that?' It struck me then that the opening repertoire of every player is much more than just the variations in his notebook (paper or digital). A big part of it is implicit, bound up in the player's personality, in the strange links he makes with other games, in contacts with other players he's played or even inspirational texts from movies or songs! Joel didn't have access to my context for the opening, and so he saw problems in completely different things to me in my openings.

This digression is my attempt to explain what you are getting with *Dynamic Chess Strategy*. You're getting the unabridged story of how Suba sees chess, complete with the personal context – anecdotes, stories, asides and sometimes seemingly unrelated comparisons that add up to a complete way of seeing chess. That way of seeing chess is not necessarily 100% consistent, and not even necessarily 100% correct, but has worked wonderfully well for Suba and is therefore extremely valuable. What you can learn from it depends for me on how closely Suba's approach matches your approach, and also – where that is not the case – how easily you can put aside your own way of doing things and spend some thoughtful time mulling over his comments. That last one is the difficult one of course, which is where my 'long quiet weekend' suggestion comes in!

Let me give you some examples. It starts with the Foreword, where a sentence made me both smile and think 'Yes that's clever', quickly followed by 'Is it clever, or does it just sound good?': 'The option to choose between a good position that cannot be improved and a bad position that can be substantially improved is also quite modern'.

I still don't quite know what I think, to be honest! This feeling continues into the first chapter, when a subsection entitled 'The Chicken or the Egg' starts off with an Eastern Euro-

Dynamic Chess Strategy by Mihai Suba New In Chess, 2016
★★★☆☆

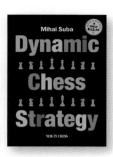

pean joke and then poses the question 'Which comes first, positional considerations or finding the next best move?' It wasn't a question that had really occurred to me before, so before even continuing I had to think about whether I thought it was a useful question or not (I'm still not sure!). Or at a later stage in the chapter about strategy, Suba remarks that 'classical strategy presupposes that you play with much weaker (or much stronger!) opponents... Strategy must

> 'It struck me then that the opening repertoire of every player is much more than just the variations in his notebook.'

show us how to fight against players of our own strength and how to make progress'. Again, I'm not sure I agree, and I'm also not sure how useful it is to spend energy discussing this.

And here we come back to my remark about my mood while reviewing the book. As I progressed through the book, I found myself grabbing more and more at the annotated games (many of which are fantastic – take a look at Suba-Pasman, Beer-Sheva 1984, a g3 Benko in which Black's king comes out to e6 by

move 14! How often does that happen?) and the concrete opening tips about the Hedgehog, while paying less and less attention to the abstract and philosophical considerations as above. Essentially I didn't get into the heart of the book at all – I'm quite frustrated about that, but I guess this wasn't the right time for me.

Difficult to give this book a star rating. I will go with a 3, and promise myself that I will pick up the book again some time later and give it another go. If I suddenly 'get it', I promise I'll come back and let you know! I will just leave you though with that great game I mentioned earlier!

Mihai Suba
Michael Pasman
Beer-Sheva 1984

1.d4 ♘f6 2.c4 c5 3.d5 b5 4.cxb5 a6 5.bxa6 g6 6.g3 ♗g7 7.d6 A risky attempt to exploit Black's unusual move order (6...d6 is usually played). **7...♕a5+ 8.♗d2 ♕xa6 9.dxe7 ♕b7 10.♘f3 ♘e4 11.♘c3 ♕xb2 12.♘xe4 ♕xa1 13.♘d6+ ♔xe7 14.♗g5+ ♔e6**

15.♗h3+ f5 16.0-0 ♕xd1 17.♖xd1 White still has an attack despite the exchange of queens. The computer is – as Suba shows – not amazingly impressed, but in the heat of the battle, Black was unable to find his way through the complications. **17...♗a6 18.e4 ♗d4 19.♗f4 ♔f6 20.exf5 ♗e2 21.♗g5+ ♔g7 22.♘xd4 h6** The only way to go! 22...♗xd1 23.f6+ ♔g8 24.♗e6+ dxe6 25.f7+ ♔f8 26.♘xe6 mate.

ANALYSIS DIAGRAM

An absolute work of art!
23.f6+ ♔g8 24.♘xe2 hxg5 25.♗g2 ♖a6 26.♘c3 g4 27.♘ce4 ♖h5 28.f7+ ♔g7 29.♘f6 ♖h8 30.♘xg4 ♖xa2 31.♘e5 ♖a4 32.♗e4 ♘c6 33.♘e8+ ♔h6 34.♘g4+ ♔g5 35.f4+ 1-0.

■ ■ ■

The sequel to *Improve Your Chess Pattern Recognition*, called *Train Your Chess Pattern Recognition* by Arthur van de Oudeweetering (New In Chess), is by contrast a very easy book to read through and gives you a very pleasant feeling of learning new things without spending too much effort! I thought that the content in this book was a little less even than the first volume. Themes work the best as a learning tool when the scope is clearly and narrowly defined and reinforced by several closely-related examples. In a number of themes I was struggling to find more than a superficial link between the positions. For example, in 'Lost without a queen' later on in the book, a chapter devoted to middlegames without queens, the first three examples are as follows:

Gligoric-Shaked
Cannes 1998
position after 13...♘xf6

Kaiumov-Inarkiev
Alushta 2002
position after 20...d5

21.g5 hxg5 22.♕xg5 And now Black should have exchanged off queens with 22...♕xg5 though his position remains difficult as his pieces are uncomfortably bunched on the queenside and his centre is under pressure. **22...dxe4 23.dxe4 ♘d8 24.♖d1 c5 25.♖d6 ♕xg5+ 26.♘xg5 ♗c7 27.♖g6 ♔h8 28.♖xg7 ♖e8 29.♗xf7** 1-0.

Romario Sanches
Yannick Pelletier
Istanbul Olympiad 2012

1.e4 d6 2.d4 ♘f6 3.♘c3 e5 4.dxe5 dxe5 5.♕xd8+ ♔xd8

... which the much higher-rated player won comfortably.

I couldn't really get a grip on the point of this chapter: a passing similarity doesn't make a good theme! However, there is also plenty of good stuff. The book begins – with typical good manners – with two themes involving the queen. Réti's idea of exerting pressure on the centre from the corner with ♕a1 gets the neat name 'Réti's Rifle' and

the author digs up a number of nice examples, of which this was definitely my favourite:

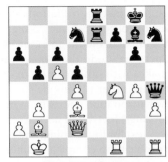

Rustemov-Postny
Bundesliga 2012
position after 26.♔b1

26...♘g5 27.♕g2 ♘e4 28.♖hg1 ♕h8

As a little aside, I was looking through some of Alekhine's games, and I came across this lovely little manoeuvre. A slight variation on 'Réti's Rifle' ... what should we call it? We already have Alekhine's Gun!

Alekhine-Grob
Bern 1932
position after 12....♘xd5

13.♕b1 f5 14.a3 ♔h8 15.♕a2

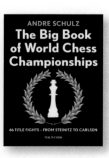

15...♘db4 16.axb4 ♘xb4 17.♕b1 f4 18.♘e5 ♗f5 19.♕d1

And White's manoeuvre ♕d1-b1-a2-b1-d1 had achieved the desired effect!

I'm in between 3 and 4 stars for this one, but I think we'll make it 4 purely for the ease of reading and learning!

■ ■ ■

The Big Book of World Chess Championships by Andre Schulz (New In Chess) is again a nice easy book to read when you're not in the mood for complicated concepts and abstract reasoning. It's actually a chess book with very little chess! As the author explains, 'Here it is not the games which are in the foreground and also not the course of the contests but rather what was happening beside the board: what were the venues and what were the circumstances for the World Championship encounters? Under what conditions and according to what rules were they played? What plots were

'A nice easy book to read when you're not in the mood for complicated concepts and abstract reasoning.'

hatched before and during the competitions?' I'm not at all qualified as a historian to comment on the accuracy of the material, but it does make for an entertaining and interesting read. The author has uncovered lots of little facts that made me at least say 'Well I never!' Such as the fact that Boris Spassky's sister Iraida Spasskaya won the Russian draughts championship four times! The weakness of the book lies in the very nature of the concept. At the end of the day, the thrill of the World Championship does lie in the way the matches developed and by dealing so summarily with this aspect, you do feel that you are missing out a bit on the essence of the whole thing. However, I read it from cover to cover with great pleasure and there is still plenty to enjoy!

■ ■ ■

And finally just room to squeeze in *Kotronias on the King's Indian Volume 4. Classical Systems* by Vassilios Kotronias (Quality Chess). It's a typi-cally dense, well-researched examination of systems such as the Exchange KID, Petrosian System, 6.h3 and the Averbakh. Looking at the lines that Kotronias recommends, it's an interesting mix of old and new. I was surprised to recognise a variation from my preparation in the early 1990s when I played the 7.♗e3 system regularly against the KID:

1.d4 ♘f6 2.c4 g6 3.♘c3 ♗g7 4.e4 d6 5.♘f3 0-0 6.♗e2 e5 7.♗e3 c6 8.0-0 exd4 9.♗xd4 ♖e8 10.♕c2 ♕e7 11.♖fe1 ♘bd7 12.h3 ♗h6 13.♖ad1 ♘e5 14.b4 b6 15.c5 ♘xf3+ 16.♗xf3 bxc5 17.bxc5 dxc5 18.♗e3 ♗xe3 19.♖xe3 ♕e5 20.♘a4

I'd assessed this as a slight edge for White. Kotronias just gives 20...c4 as equal. I guess the idea is 21.♕xc4 ♗e6. It might have been handy to analyse this a little further, as it's pretty crucial for the evaluation of the line. Little gripes like this aside, the thoroughness of Kotronias' research is very impressive. He even dedicates a whole chapter to the line 5.♗e2 0-0 6.♗e3 e5 7.d5 with the idea of a quick g4-g5, which was another of my favourites in the early 1990s! A must for any budding KID player! ■

Fischer vs

Heroes of their time. In 1972, on his return from Reykjavik, Bobby Fischer was honoured by New York Mayor John Lindsay.

After he had lost the world title, Bobby Fischer often wallowed in denigrating remarks about the games and game comments of his successor Anatoly Karpov. Did the American have a point? A great admirer of both players, **MIHAIL MARIN**, subjected Karpov's games to fresh analysis, looking for the truth, even though he feared that one of his heroes might fall off his pedestal.

To many of his fans, and not only them, Bobby Fischer's return to tournament chess in the second half of the '70s seemed imminent. As the last dethroned World Champion, Fischer had the right to compete in the 1977 Candidates' matches without needing to go through the Interzonals. But the arguably greatest player in history did not show up and his place was taken by Spassky, whom he had defeated in

1972. With great regret, Fischer's fans (including yours truly) had to admit that their hero had become a thing of the past, quite a glorious one, but still of the past...

And yet, I recently found out that my secret hopes were not entirely unjustified. In his *Duels with the World Champions*, Yasser Seirawan writes that years after having lost his title, Fischer was still carefully ana-

lysing Karpov's games. Fischer displayed his sharpest irony when finding mistaken moves or analysis of the one he referred to as 'the so-called World Champion Karpitch'!

I read this with mixed feelings. We all need idols, models and heroes, but how should we deal with the situation when two of them get into creative rivalry and even controversy? Fischer and Karpov were both heroes to me.

FISCHER-KARPOV

'Karpov rarely attaches question marks to his moves, signalling only the moments when his opponent was not up to the challenge.'

Karpov

Whose side was I to take, who should I believe?

I have always regarded Fischer as the perfect player, which for many years stopped me from studying his games in detail, fearing that getting too close to the sun would make my wax wings melt, as in the old Icarus myth... But Fischer's perfection also offered me the hope that there is practically no human limit for a chess player's achievements, which has been quite an inspiring feeling all through my career

With Karpov, things were different. After giving up hope that my other great hero, Kortchnoi, could defeat him in a world title match, I accepted that Karpov was in a way stronger and that there was actually a lot to be learned from his games and comments.

To me, the most instructive thread in Karpov's play was the tight connection between strategy and tactics, the elegance of the concrete conversion of an accumulated positional advantage when the position was

ripe for it. Karpov had the tendency to present his wins as single logical sequences, which used to be Akiba Rubinstein's trademark. Karpov rarely attaches question marks to his moves, signalling only the moments when his opponent was not up to the challenge.

But after reading the Fischer episode I started fearing that many of the games that had served me as a guide during my teen-age were in fact flawed.

With great fervour, I started revisiting some of my old favourites, taking as a principle that I should discover any mistakes without the computer and use the only analysing tool available to Fischer in the late '70s – the tri-dimensional board. When I embarked on this project, I feared that the final result would make me lose at least one idol. If Fischer was right, then much of what I had learned from Karpov could be worthless, but if he was wrong, then my belief in the achievability of perfection would be destroyed.

I feel fortunate that neither of these things happened. After double-checking my personal analysis with the engines, I came to the paradoxical conclusion that I could safely keep both statues on their high pedestals.

Before exemplifying the sometimes imperceptible spots on the sun, I will examine one of Karpov's most instructive games, showing him at his best from the perspective I had many decades ago.

Karpov-Spassky
Moscow 1973
position after 23.♗xc4

White is perfectly mobilized, but

even though Black is lagging some-what in development, his regrouping is harmonious, too. In order to equalize, Black only needs to get rid of his backward pawn with ...c7-c5, but there are some concrete details to deal with first.

23...♕e7? Karpov rightly criticized this move, suggesting 23...♘xc4 24.♕xc4 as the lesser evil. As an experienced Ruy Lopez specialist with both colours, Spassky understood, of course, that leaving the Spanish bishop on the board was risky, but he probably feared that clearing the c-file for the white queen would make it difficult for him to carry out his plan. In fact, after 24...♖c8 25.♗e3, 25...♕e7, followed by ...♗f8 and inevitably ...c5, would offer Black good play.

24.♗b3! The most obvious and strongest move.

The engines prefer the bishop retreats along the f1-a6 diagonal, probably underestimating Karpov's exchange sacrifice. Be that as it may, 24.♗f1 frees Black of any worries along the a2-g8 diagonal, allowing him to regroup with 24...♘f8, followed by ...♘e6, with acceptable play.

24...c5 The most active plan, aiming to neutralize the active bishop.

After 24...♘f8 25.h4, Black will have problems on the light squares.

25.a4! The start of a well-calculated forced sequence, designed by Karpov on the previous move.

25...c4 Karpov analyses 25...cxb4 26.a5 ♖ac8 27.♕a2 ♘a8 28.♗xb4!.

26.♗a2 ♗c6

The point behind Black's plan. Other-

wise a4-a5 would simply win the c4-pawn.

27.a5 ♗a4 28.♕c1

So far, the main events have taken part on the queenside, but the last move marks a sudden switch to the other wing. Short queen moves are likely to change the course of the game radically, as witness, for instance, Alekhine's 21.♕e2-d2 in the famous 34th and last game of his match against Capablanca.

28...♘c8 29.♗xh6 ♗xd1 30.♖xd1

Both players must have reached this position in their calculations when embarking on the forced line. White has a pawn for the exchange and needs to get the c4-pawn as well in order to claim a positional advantage. But Spassky thought he had seen one move further:

30...♘d6? He obviously thought that his knights were invulnerable in view of 31.♗xg7 ♔xg7 32.♕d2? ♘f6 33.♕xd6? ♖ad8 and Black wins. Had he anticipated Karpov's 32nd move, he would have chosen 30...♘f6 or 30...♘f8, with just a clearly worse position.

31.♗xg7 ♔xg7

32.♕g5!!

The decisive move, threatening not only 33.♕xe7, followed by 34.♖xd6, but also 33.♖xd6, followed by 34.♘f5+.

32...f6

The only way to avoid material losses, but it weakens the kingside too much.

33.♕g4 ♔h7 34.♘h4!

It is not hard to establish that Black is helpless against the combined attack of the white pieces, so Spassky resigned, just a couple of moves after thinking that he had out-tricked his younger opponent.

I failed to find any flaw in this game and, after some hesitation, the engines also confirmed that Karpov's play was perfect. Quite probably, Fischer had nothing to object to and might have been even a bit jealous of Karpov's achievement.

This type of combinatory play on both wings, with strategy and tactics going hand in hand, is one of Karpov's trademark qualities: the uniquely subtle feel for the global harmony of his position. But in the next game we will see a similar scenario marred by imperfection.

Karpov-Gligoric
Leningrad 1973
position after 25...♘e8

Due to his bishop pair Black's position looks fine strategically, but the main question is whether White will be able to conjure up an advantage out of his massive control of the a-file before Black manages to neutralize it by exchanges.

Gligoric' last move was 25...♘f6-e8, preparing wholesale exchanges with ...♘c7 and ...♖a8.

26.♕a6!

The most precise move, even though it seems to be playing straight into Black's hands.

26.♕a5 would help Black regroup his minor pieces: 26...♕xa5 (simpler and slightly stronger than Karpov's suggestion 26...♕c8, followed by ...♗d8) 27.♖1xa5 ♗d8 28.♖5a6 ♗c8, when Black would have little to fear.

26...♖b6!

Since the rook is exposed on b6, this will actually lose a tempo for Black, but it still is Black's best defence.

It must have been painful for Gligoric to refrain from the planned 26...♘c7 27.♕a5 ♖a8. Unlike Spassky when he played 30...♘d6?, the former world title candidate managed to spot Karpov's devilish idea: 28.♖xa8 (28.♕b6 achieves little after 28...♕b8, followed by ...♖c8 and ...♗d8. The knight is taboo, since the a7-rook is pinned) 28...♕xa8 29.♕xc7!. Another exchange sacrifice combined with a switch to the kingside. True, this time the queen will need several tempi to reach an attacking position. 29...♕xa1+ 30.♔h2 ♖d8 31.♗xb5! ♗xb5 32.♕xe7 ♖d7. Just as

in the previous game, the introductory queenside play has resulted into the possibility of starting an attack with queen and knights against the poorly defended king. Black's queen is far away and the bishop is vulnerable and faces being restricted with c3-c4.

ANALYSIS DIAGRAM

Both players had calculated this line, but now their ways diverge. During the post-mortem, Gligoric confessed that he had been afraid of 33.♘f5+, but Karpov thought this would not yield more than a draw. Their joint analysis seems to have convinced Gligoric that his younger opponent was right, since in his comments for *Chess Informant* he only analyses 33.♕h4. Karpov evaluated that he would have enough compensation for the sacrificed exchange and planned to continue with either 33.♕g5 or 33.♕h4, 'with good attacking chances'.

It is hard to predict what would have happened if the game had actually gone this way, but since this variation remained backstage, Karpov did

not feel like examining this position in detail, neither in his initial comments for the Soviet magazine *64*, nor in his successive editions of his selected games.

I must confess that the complexity of the position proved too great for my 'hand-made' analytical abilities. I 'believed' Karpov that 33.♘f5+ was ineffective, but clearly preferred 33.♕g5 over 33.♕h4.

Computer analysis provided surprising conclusions, which I have tried to sum up as schematically as possible. The reason why I discarded 33.♕h4 was that it apparently creates only one big threat – 34.♘g4.

ANALYSIS DIAGRAM

Things are in fact not that simple, but Black can save the day with 33...♕xc3!!.

(Gligoric analyses 33...f6 34.c4 ♗a6 35.♘g4, 'with a clear advantage', but White is actually winning. My try was 33...♕c1, defending the h6-square in advance, but White wins with 34.c4, forcing the bishop to leave the a4-e8 diagonal: 34...♗a6 35.♘g5 h6 36.♘e6+! fxe6 37.dxe6 ♖a7 38.♕d8. Since the bishop no longer controls e8, the pawn is unstoppable and Black will achieve little with ...♕d2 and ...♕xf2.)

The last move in the main line ensures the bishop's stability, allowing Black to parry the threats in time after 34.♘g4 ♕c1, when White should already be looking for a perpetual.

Gligoric's initial intuition was right, since 33.♘f5+! gxf5 34.♕g5+ is the most convincing win.

ANALYSIS DIAGRAM

During the post-mortem both players must have overlooked that any king retreat would be met by ♘h4, a quiet but lethal move. White will soon have a lot of pawns for the rook and his attack would retrieve at least an exchange. Here are just two illustrative lines: 34...♔h8 (or if 34...♔f8 35.♘h4 f6, clearing some space around the king: 36.♕xf6+ ♖f7 37.♕xd6+ ♔g8 38.♘xf5) 35.♘h4 f6 (a familiar picture) 36.♕xf6+ ♔g8 37.♘xf5 h5 38.♕g6+ ♔f8 39.♕xh5 (threatening 40.♕h8+ followed by mate in two) 39...♔g8 40.♕g5+ ♔h7 41.c4!?. Black cannot withdraw his bishop due to ♕h5+ and ♕e8+, winning the rook.

Karpov's first suggestion of 33.♕g5!, threatening both ♘f5+ and ♘g4, also wins, but it turns out that it leads to a slightly worsened version of the attack after 33.♘f5+. Gligoric must have discarded it in his analysis because of the forced 33...f6,

ANALYSIS DIAGRAM

which will not save him: 34.♘f5+ ♔f7 (or if 34...♔g8 35.♕xf6 gxf5 36.♕e6+ ♔f8 37.c4, White wins the bishop, while Black's counterplay is

rather volatile: 37...♕c1 38.cxb5 ♕f4+ 39.♔h1 ♕c1+ 40.♘g1 ♖d8 41.exf5, with three pawns for the exchange and a continuing attack) 35.♕h6 ♔g8

ANALYSIS DIAGRAM

36.♘3h4!!. The only winning move, leading to a familiar attacking pattern. The immediate threat is 37.♘xg6. 36...gxf5 37.♘xf5 ♖f7 38.♘xd6. Black has

> 'A critical mind like Fischer's would suspect that Karpov omitted this idea in his comments on purpose.'

to give up his bishop, leaving White with two pawns for the exchange and a clear positional advantage. Otherwise he would lose quickly: 38...♗a6 (or, if 38...♗d7, then 39.♘xf7 ♔xf7 40.♕xh7+ ♔e8 41.d6 ♔d8 42.♕h8+! ♗e8 43.♕xf6+ ♔c8 44.♕f8 and wins) 39.♘xf7 ♔xf7. Now White could get the fourth pawn for the bishop or go for the immediate 40.d6!?, when 40...♔e6 fails to stop the pawn due to 41.♕f8, winning.

Understanding the full strength of the attack based on ♘h4-f5 is not within everyone's reach, and both players seem to have underestimated it when

writing their comments. My wild guess is that Tal would have gone for it without too much hesitation, just because it felt right and it promised a lot of fun. Even though Fischer's style was more rounded-up than Tal's, his attacking skills were famous and I believe there is a fair chance he would have discovered the effectiveness of this idea.

But all these considerations do not make Karpov's and Gligoric' comments less instructive. The main thing to retain is the gradual transition from positional queenside play to a tactical kingside attack.

27.♕a5 Threatening 28.♖xd7.
27...♘f6

Black has defended his hanging bishop and plans to regroup with ...♕b8 and ...♖b7. White needs some radical measures to try and keep the initiative.

28.♘g4!?
Abstractly speaking, the same approach as in the lines above – White intends to develop his queenside initiative with a blow on the opposite wing. The threat is 29.♘xf6, followed by 30.♖xd7, while 28...♘xg4? loses the b5-pawn after 29.♖xd7! ♕xd7 30.♕xb6 with a clear white advantage.

28...♖b8? Justifying White's previous play. This kind of little tempo game involving moves like ♕a2-a6-a5, ...♖b8-b6-b8 and ...♘f6-e8-f6 is typical for Karpov, showing once more his sense of overall harmony.

But it is curious that neither player mentions the simplest solution to

Black's problems: 28...♗xg4! 29.hxg4. Black has exchanged the hanging bishop for the molesting knight, but still needs to parry the threat of ♖xe7. His b5-pawn is hanging, but so are the g4- and e4-pawns.

ANALYSIS DIAGRAM

The modest 29...♖b8!? would yield Black an entirely viable position, since 30.♗xb5 will lose an exchange to 30...♛xa5 31.♖1xa5 ♗d8. Or if 30.g5, then 30...♘g4 31.♖a6, indirectly defending g5: 31...♛xa5 32.♖6xa5 c4 33.bxc4 bxc4 34.♗xc4 ♖fc8, possibly followed by ...♖b2. Moreover, he can carry out the pawn break at once: 29...c4! 30.bxc4 bxc4 31.♗xc4 ♘xg4, since 32.♖xe7? is impossible due to 32...♖b1+ 33.♗f1 ♖xa1 34.♛xa1 ♛xe7 and Black wins. As much as I would like to, I cannot take the credit for these lines and I cannot even put them on my engine. All hints are paradoxically given by... Karpov himself in his comments to the next move!

29.♘xf6

Karpov writes that the tempting 29.♛c7 would run into 29...♗xg4 30.hxg4 ♛xc7 31.♖xc7 ♗d8 32.♖c6 c4 33.bxc4 bxc4 34.♖xc4 ♘xg4, with counterplay. Does all this look familiar?!

This brings up a series of questions. Why does Karpov not mention the similar line when it was Black's choice to go for it? Quite possibly, he played 28.♘g4 without thinking twice, since there was virtually no other hope for an advantage, so he might not have had the time to evaluate 28...♗xg4

properly. But things changed later, when he refrained from 29.♛c7.

A critical mind like Fischer's would suspect that Karpov omitted this idea in his comments on purpose, in order to present the game as perfect. I would not be surprised if this was true, since it was the only politically correct approach in the Soviet Union. As for Gligoric, he must have been demoralized after failing to make 26...♘c7 work, thinking that Karpov had outplayed him. In such cases one tends to become 'cooperative' with moves like 28...♖b8.

After the game move Karpov's pressure develops naturally.

29...♗xf6

30.♛c7 ♛xc7 31.♖xc7 ♖fd8 32.♖aa7 ♗e8 33.♖ab7 ♔g8 34.g4

Black is paralysed and Karpov won 30 moves later.

Except from the vague feeling that Karpov was not entirely sincere in his comments, I do not find any significant flaws in this game. Black committed only one major inaccuracy on move 28, but chess is not only a science, but also a fighting game. In other words, if Fischer referred to these games in his chats, he was basically right, but it looks more as if he was searching for spots on the sun. No interior psychological trouble for me so far; both idols stand!

The next example features a different picture, strongly inclining the balance into Fischer's favour. This contrast is symbolically increased by the

fact that this time Karpov switched his focus in the opposite direction: from the kingside and centre to the queenside.

Karpov-Miles
London 1982
position after 22.♖d4

In those years I was strongly tempted to include the Dragon and the Pirc in my repertoire, and I even filled two notebooks with games and analysis in these openings. I had Anthony Miles as a model for the Dragon, as he was the player who managed to revive this controversial variation in the late 1970s.

However, I was inhibited by Karpov's constant success with his positional (= boring) systems against these openings, and it was not until 12 years later that I started playing them in official games. I believe that I was helped by the fact that Karpov had meanwhile switched to 1.d4; without their main slayer around, the Dragon and the Pirc started looking playable again.

I remember how frustrating this game was for me as a teenager. When I first saw this position, I thought that Black could not hope for more in the positional Dragon: his knight is more versatile than the bishop, the d5-pawn is at least as weak as the e7-pawn and Black has a pleasant minority attack. And yet, Miles got smashed quite convincingly, at least judging from Karpov's comments. When looking anew at the position with an experienced eye, I tried to convince my 'younger self' that his perception was incomplete. White has more space for and chances of a kingside attack, while his rooks are admirably placed, in genuine Karpov style.

As 'the two of us' started playing through the endgame, the teenager in me remained reluctant to accept much of my mature preaching, and in the comments below I have inserted his childish answers between quotation marks.

22...a5

Karpov criticizes this move and recommends 22...♞a4, followed by ...♞b6, in order to tie White to the defence of the d5-pawn. If we spice up this plan with doubling rooks on the c-file, it becomes obvious that White would not have enough resources to increase his kingside pressure.

According to Karpov, Miles had underestimated the weakening of his queenside caused by his last move.

23.b4

Being better mobilized, White can afford to react on the wing where Black was dreaming to start his attack. Miles will soon regret having weakened his b5-pawn so light-heartedly.

'But White's queenside weaknesses look even uglier, and besides, Black has regrouped well, too.'

23...♞a4

Karpov assesses the position after 23...axb4 24.♜xb4 as better for White. I did not react to my alter ego's sceptical look for once, as I could not find any way to strengthen the pressure after 24...♜cb7. Moreover, Black is threatening to set up a drawing

mechanism: 25...♞a6 26.♜be4 ♚f8, followed by 27...♞c5, when in order to prevent ...b5-b4, with initiative, White would have to agree to a draw by repetition with 28.♜b4.

24.bxa5

This pawn is not dangerous yet, but Black should not underestimate its force while carrying out his counterplay.

24...♞c3 25.♗f1 ♚f8?!

Karpov gives 25...♜a8 26.♚b2 ♞a4+ 27.♚b3 ♞c5+ 28.♚b4, with the implicit evaluation that White is better. After incorporating the king in the attack, White is practically playing with an extra piece.

ANALYSIS DIAGRAM

'But isn't it just a forced draw by repetition after 28...♞a6+!. White would do better to refrain from 29.♚xb5? ♜b7+ 30.♚c4 (30.♚c6 ♞c5 traps the king, forcing White to give up material for questionable compensation: 31.♜xe7 ♜xe7 32.♚xd6 ♜e4!?) 30...♞c5. Black will soon retrieve both a-pawns, with an obvious positional advantage.'

By this time I felt that the world had started falling apart around my ears. If I had analysed this and similar games more carefully, I could have started playing the Dragon and the Pirc ages before I did. I started wondering if I would ever be able to forgive myself for getting inhibited for so many years. I felt comforted, though, by the feeling that I could finally reconcile myself with my younger me. 'The wiser one always steps back,' I proudly told my present self.

26.♚b2

Karpov's comment is instructive: 'Black's aim is to place one rook on c5 and the other on the a-file, but he will not manage to carry out this plan.' Abstractly, this is very insightful, but the World Champion underestimated Black's dynamism somewhat.

26...♜bc8?

The knight will now remain tied to the defence of the b5-pawn. As we will see, Miles's plan to get the d5-pawn is flawed. 26...♞a4+ would still have offered chances of equality.

27.♚b3 ♜c5 28.a6

Taking advantage of Miles's lack of resolution, Karpov manages to implement his plan. Suddenly, this pawn becomes dangerous, and the World Champion has planned a devilish refutation to Black's natural answer.

28...♞xd5 29.♜xd5!

The abstract idea is simple: White clears the long diagonal, planning ♗g2, followed by the advance of the a-pawn. But there are some concrete details to be worked out and Karpov will deal with them brilliantly.

29...♜xd5

30.♖c3!!

Attacking the back-rank defender and causing problems with the return into play of the d5-rook.

After the hurried 30.♗g2?, Black retrieves his harmony with 30...♖d4, followed by ...♖a4, with approximate equality.

30...♖d8

30...♖xc3+ 31.♔xc3 ♖c5+ 32.♔b4 ♖c7 33.♗g2 wins (Karpov).

31.♖c7

The simplest. Even though the pawn material is equal, Black's extra exchange is not worth much. His rooks do not communicate, making the a-pawn unstoppable.

31...♖d1 32.♗xb5 e5 33.a7 exf4 34.♖b7 ♖b1+ 35.♔a4 ♖xb5 36.♖xb5 f3 37.♖b8 f2 38.♖xd8+ 1-0.

Due to space limitations I have inserted only a few of the Karpov games I went through recently. They illustrate three different categories:
1. A flawless game showing Karpov at his best, both as a player and an annotator;
2. A great game from many points of view, but with an important flaw, which Karpov seems to have swept under the carpet;
3. A fighting game in which Karpov's resolute play eventually confused his opponent. His comments on the initial phase are over-optimistic, but maybe it was precisely this self-confidence that offered him an additional advantage during the game. When the position was ripe for it, Karpov carried out his winning manoeuvre in flawless fashion.

How would I then solve the thematic conflict between my heroes? Whose side should I take?

I feel fortunate that after this analytical excursion both Fischer and Karpov kept or even strengthened their position in my scale of values. In his quest for perfection, Fischer does not content himself with just 'instructive games'. For him, every single piece of the puzzle has to stand in the right place, no matter if in over the board play or analysis.

Karpov is less diligent from this point of view, but his patterns of global strategic thinking are instructive even when illustrated by imperfect games.

And my wildest dream is to play a game with Karpov's apparent ease, based on Fischer's perfect accuracy... ∎

A scholar of beauty

A remark by Hikaru Nakamura rekindled **HANS REE**'s enthusiasm for a book on chess beauty by François Le Lionnais (1901-1984), a French writer with a universal intellectual appetite.

L ast year I wrote a column about shedding half of my library, which was painful at the time. Meanwhile I have experienced the silver lining. Just by being moved, the books that I had selected to accompany me to my new, smaller apartment gained a new lease of life. Books that I had forgotten about, books that in the past I had only browsed or not read at all, had different locations on the shelves now and seemed like new acquisitions. It seemed as if I had more books to read, both about chess and about other things, than before the great purge.

One of these was *Les Prix de Beauté aux Échecs* (the beauty prizes in chess) by François Le Lionnais. I use the expression beauty prize here, because it is a more general concept than brilliancy prize. It is a big book. My copy, a second edition from 1951, has 508 pages, about a hundred of which are devoted to a detailed investigation of the question: What makes a game beautiful? Le Lionnais is very strict with his seven conditions that a game has to fulfill to be worthy of a beauty prize. In 1939, when the first edition of his book appeared, he could not know that computers would eventually show that very few games actually live up to his standards.

Beauty is in the eye of the beholder,

and the greater the chess knowledge of the observer, the more fastidious he will be when it comes to recognizing beauty. We no longer see much beauty in ♗xh7+, except when there is a surprising new twist, as in Nepomniachtchi-Sjugirov from the recent Russian team championship: 10.♗xh7+ ♔xh7, and now, not the banal 11.♘g5+, but the unexpected 11.h4, with a large advantage for White. Beautiful, but next time it will already be old hat.

In a recent *New York Times* article Hikaru Nakamura was quoted: 'If you talk to some of the older players, they definitely say they see beauty in certain games. In my case, there are times when I think, "Wow, that's so amazing; chess is so full of ideas." But most of the time I tend to be more pragmatic about it, as opposed to thinking about it as art or something exquisite.'

Beauty as a romantic concept of older players, that sounds bleak. But the divide is not absolute, of course. I have never met an older player who would prefer a beautiful loss to a run-of-the-mill win. They were pragmatic, too. Nevertheless there might be a real difference between the older players and Nakamura's generation.

In 2013, when the American magazine *MISC*, which describes itself as a journal of insight and foresight about design, business and inno-

vation, asked Magnus Carlsen how he and his colleagues thought about style, he answered: 'For me, more than style, the main thing is to try to make the best move in any position. Having preferences regarding a certain style can be a weakness, as you need to cope with any position. That said, most people have certain preferences.'

Dubious beauty

Apparently, the first brilliancy prize in history was awarded in 1876. It was given to Henry Bird for his victory over James Mason in a tournament in New York. White sacrificed a pawn, an exchange and then his queen for a rook and a knight.

The pawn sacrifice with which it all began receives two exclamation marks from Le Lionnais. Playing over the game with Stockfish 7 running, I saw that the move should in fact have led to a quick loss. Later in the game, Le Lionnais systematically underestimates Mason's chances with queen against rook and knight. By his own criteria, the game, however spectacular, should never have won a prize, but he couldn't know that in the pre-computer age.

Le Lionnais was a good player, but not a great one. But Reuben Fine, who annotated Bird's game in his book *The World's Great Chess Games*, didn't do any better in his own annotations.

Nakamura, Carlsen and other players of their generation have worked so often with computers that their chess instincts may have become similar to those of the engines. For me and most chess lovers, beauty and a recognizable style are connected. Computer games provide little beauty and hardly a recognizable style. To the present human eye, that is. At the same time, engines unmask the allure of beauty that is based on a lack of knowledge. Henry Bird's game of 1876 seems less beautiful after computer analysis.

So if we want to save beauty, it has to be beauty of a more sophisticated kind. Perhaps a kind of beauty that can only be created by the engines themselves, and only explained to humans by the engines: Chess Beauty 2.0, more akin to the beauty of nature, e.g. an intricate crystal, than to human cogitation.

I think this idea would have appealed to Le Lionnais, who was always interested in modern technology. In 1956, on behalf of Unesco, he chaired the *First International Congress on Cybernetics* in Namur, and from 1961 till 1963 he was part of a group, sponsored by Euratom and headed by Max Euwe, that investigated the mathematics of a chess machine.

Universal curiosity

François Le Lionnais was one of the most remarkable men to have put his mark on the chess world. His achievements in chess are substantial. He wrote a number of chess books, two of which are classics: the book about the beauty prizes and the *Dictionnaire des échecs* (1967, with Ernst Paget), a fine encyclopedia of chess. Between 1932 and 1938 he was owner and editor of the chess magazine *Cahiers de l'échiquier français*. But for the French his work in chess is only a minor amusement compared to his accomplishments in other fields.

He was honoured as *Commander of the Legion of Honour* and received the *Rosette of the Resistance* and the *Cross of War 1939-1940*. The list of his functions and titles, many serious and some mock-serious, is near endless.

In different stages of his life he was a chemical engineer, a writer on classic and romantic beauty in mathematics, an entrepreneur, President of the French Association of science

'Le Lionnais is very strict with his seven conditions that a game has to fulfill to be worthy of a beauty prize. He could not know that computers would eventually show that very few games actually live up to his standards.'

writers, a Communist and member of the French resistance, a concentration camp prisoner, director of general studies at the French Academy of War, scientific adviser to the French national museums and a member of the French Association of conjurors, the International Society of the Rat and the International Society Maledicta, which latter organization devoted itself to the study of insults and obscenities.

I could go on. Above all, Le Lionnais considered himself an artist.

I think he will be mostly remembered as the founder (together with a friend, the writer Raymond Queneau) of Oulipo in 1960. Oulipo stands for Ouvroir de littérature potentielle: Workplace of potential litera-ture. Members of Oulipo have been described (by themselves) as rats who build the labyrinths from which they want to escape. One literary masterpiece it spawned is *La Vie mode d'emploi* (Life, a User's Manual) by Georges Perec. The organizing principle of that book is the knight's tour.

A camp in Germany

Chess may have saved Le Lionnais's life. In November 1944 he was arrested and, after having been tortured, deported to the German camp Dora-Mittelbau. It was not an extermination camp, since the prisoners had to work on the new V2 rocket, the 'Vergeltungswaffe' that was supposed to win the war for Germany, but many inmates died, from execution, illness or exhaustion.

Every day, Le Lionnais got a piece of paper to wipe his bottom. One day he found that his paper of the day contained a fragment of a chess column he had written. This led to a better understanding with a German guard, who began to ask his advice about positions from his own games against other guards. Then Le Lionnais began to receive Red Cross parcels and was given access to books and even allowed to write a chess book. His handcuffs were removed.

In April 1945, Le Lionnais, together with some other inmates, managed to escape from a death march. They reached the neighbouring village of Seesen, where the Nazi authorities had realized that their game was up. Le Lionnais managed to find paper and a press to produce a one-issue newspaper on May 5th, called *Revivre!* (To live again!) A short article headlined 'Hitler is dead!' was accompanied by a photograph with the caption: 'The famous comedian Hitler in his role as Napoleon in the super-production "The retreat from Russia".'

After his return to France Le Lionnais found that he had been expelled from the Communist party, after which he would never be involved in politics again. ■

Improving Your Pieces

What do you do when 'nothing is going on'?
PARIMARJAN NEGI explains that it always
makes sense to see if there is a piece that would
be better off on another square.

I t is easy to prepare for tactics: you solve a lot of positions. In such positions there is always a best move and your job is to find it. But in real games, such situations are rare. Most of the time you just shuffle your pieces around, often choosing from different plans.

Here I will talk about situations in which there doesn't seem to be a lot of tactical stuff going on. If there aren't a lot of tactical confrontations, there is usually less pressure to play accurately. This is tricky, because it is still very important to keep your pieces on good squares. This may sound obvious, but the simplest positional rules are often the toughest to follow.

First of all, why is this important? Because almost inevitably, tactical clashes will arise, when the placement of your pieces will be as important as your calculating abilities. In tactical puzzles, your pieces are always placed perfectly. But in a game, it is your responsibility to make sure that they are placed just right.

Usually it is perfectly acceptable to trust your intuition when deciding how to continue. But before you actually make your move, you should always consider the following question: ***Does my move make any of my pieces worse?***

This might seem like an obvious observation, but it is very easy to forget about this when you are thinking about other plans, as we will see in the next game.

Rapport-Grandelius
Abu Dhabi 2015
position after 17...♗d6

Rapport's typical aggressive pawns on both sides haven't achieved much, and now it was perhaps time to think about equality, exchange a few pieces perhaps. But that's not the young Hungarian's style... Instead he shut down his own bishop with **18.f4?** I can't really think of a good reason for keeping the g3-bishop – particularly after Black's next pawn push, when it is basically dead.
18...h5! 19.g5 g6 Just making sure that the ♗g3 doesn't get a second lease of life any time soon.
20.e4 OK, the bishop can actually come out from f2 – but that opens the position more, which doesn't look too good for his king.
20...dxe4 21.♕xe4 ♕c7 22.♗f2

22.0-0 would have been a perfectly good move. But there isn't any hurry, and what black piece can be easily improved?

22...♘e7! This was not hard to guess. I wonder, though, if Grandelius realized that he would lose the a7-pawn here? It's easy to overlook, of course, but his position just looks so pleasant – particularly his superior knight, compared to White's useless pieces – that it doesn't matter in the least.
23.♗xa7 0-0 24.♗d4 ♘f5 25.♖h3 ♖fe8 26.♗e5 ♗xe5 27.♕xe5

27...♕c6! The bad bishop is gone, but White's other pieces aren't much better. Black, on the other hand, is doing spectacularly well.

28.♔f2 ♖ed8 29.♕c5 ♕e4 30.♕e5 ♕c2 31.a5 ♖d2

Black's pieces have penetrated. In the ensuing tactics, White's uncoordinated pieces had little chance, of course.

It is much harder to actually improve your pieces than to avoid making them worse. To start with, it is very helpful to ask yourself the question: *Which of my pieces are bad? Can I improve any of them?*

Sometimes the answer to such questions is very obvious. If you can easily improve one of your pieces, then you should certainly do so, especially when you are developing.

Howell-Negi
Leiden 2012
position after 12...f6

We have a fairly balanced position here. White has many plans, and he decides to try to prepare f4. Black is ready to deal with it, so he spends some time readjusting his pieces to prepare for it.
Meanwhile, I couldn't quite see what I should be doing myself, so I just shuffled around my pieces without any plan.

'In tactical puzzles, your pieces are always placed perfectly. But in a game, it is your responsibility to make sure that they are placed just right.'

13.♔h1 ♘b8 14.♘g1 ♘c6 15.♘e2

15...♕d7

This seems like an improvement, but with ...♕d7 and ...♖ad8, etc., I had no plans. I was hoping I was still improving my pieces, but it was no good, since on d8 the rook is not really doing anything either. Instead, I should have realized that I should play something more concrete, like ...b5, which would have made it harder for White to improve his pieces.
Indeed, 15...b5! 16.axb6 cxb6 and ...♗c7 and ...b5 next would have been great, forcing White to go 17.♘xd6 ♕xd6, with an equal position.

16.♗e3 ♖ad8 17.♕d2 ♔h8 18.f3!

A crucial move. White doesn't rush to play f4, because Black is quite ready to deal with it. Instead, he continues to improve his pieces with the eventual plan of playing f4.

18...♗e7 Again, I play more or less aimlessly.

19.♖f2! This looks surprising, but doubled rooks on the f-file will certainly be useful after f4.

19...♘g8 20.♖af1 ♘d4 21.♘c3 ♕c6 Finally, I am trying to play ...b5, but I could have done this on move 15 already!

22.f4 exf4 23.♗xf4 b5 24.axb6 cxb6 25.♘e3 f5 26.♘xf5 ♘xf5 27.♗g5!

And unexpectedly, the doubled rooks on the f-file prove crucial, as after **27...♗xg5 28.♕xg5** the knight on f5 is pinned and White remains a pawn up. In the game I still managed to find some compensation, and it was a long battle before I lost.

The above example wasn't very hard. But what can you do when you are already completely developed? There are always ways to improve your pieces. One way is to think about the plan you want to follow. A particular breakthrough perhaps? Or maybe you want to start playing against some weaknesses on the queenside?

Then you have to ask yourself the question: *Am I ready for that plan? Or could I take some of my pieces to better squares, so that when I go for it, I will be in better shape?*

As I said above, when there are no immediate tactics in the position, there is much less pressure. So you do not

have to be right. Nor do you have to hurry. The important thing is that it will make you follow a plan instead of aimlessly moving your pieces.

Giri-Tomashevsky
Khanty-Mansiysk 2015 (7)
position after 23...♖ed8

The game is quite balanced, but it's hard to see how to make progress with White. A good way to think in such situations is – how can I improve my pieces?

24.♗c1! This doesn't exactly look like improving a piece, does it? As I said before, piece placement can be very subjective, but the bishop is actually doing something on c1 at least – crucially defending the b2-pawn, which Black was bound to target sooner rather than later. Nor was it doing anything on h6.

24...d5 Now White could leave the central tension for what it is, but instead he seizes the opportunity to bring his a4-rook back in the game and create more space for his pieces, at the cost of a weak d3-pawn.

25.exd5 ♕xd5 26.♖ae4! The rook is headed for e3 – from where it can easily defend the d3-pawn.

26...f6 27.♕a4!? Not exactly necessary, but one of those little moves that can be annoying for Black. A couple of moves back, Black had been doing great, but now suddenly his pieces aren't exactly ideally placed, and he doesn't have a clear plan. Meanwhile, White's pieces are well-placed, and he can continue to improve them.

27...♖bc8 28.♖4e3 ♖c7
Which white piece has not been improved yet? The rooks are fine where they are, ♗c1 isn't ideal, but it's not as if you can change it, so...

29.♘d2! The knight goes to the promised square c4, which also opens the third rank for the e3-rook to move around and annoy Black even more. Suddenly, White's pieces are looking even better. Things are still complicated – as Black's position is solid – but just seeing your opponent improve his pieces, while it's hard to do much with your own pieces, can be disconcerting.

29...♖cd7 30.♘c4 ♕e6 31.♕c2
Keeping Black's ideas under control. He is still struggling to play useful moves.

31...♗d6 After 31...♕f7 White can play 32.h4 or just slow, reinforcing moves like 32.♕e2, etc. Avoiding f4 doesn't solve all Black's problems.

32.f4 ♗c7 White has different plans here, and I wonder how clearly Anish saw his full plan when he played: **33.♖f3!?** Shuffling around. No immediate threat, but posturing with possibly improved squares for his pieces. The key is that Black cannot do much and will continue to suffer.

33...♖d5 34.♕e2 Doesn't seem to be doing much... **34...♔h8 35.♕f1!** Whoa! Suddenly the rook on f3 is perfectly placed, as White exerts pressure along the f-file and in the centre. Had he seen this when he played ♖f3? That would be pretty impressive...

35...f5 Now that the job on the f-file is done, White just continues to play slowly, aiming his pieces at other targets: **36.♖fe3 ♕f6 37.♕e2 ♖e8 38.g4!?** This might not be the strongest move objectively, but it seems troubling enough for Black. Now his position collapses.

38...♕h4 39.gxf5 gxf5 Black probably thought that because he had already played ...♔h8 he would be just fine, as White has to spend time to move his king... But after **40.♔h1!** White's pieces are far better placed to play on the newly opened kingside, whereas Black's pieces are just scattered around...

40...♖d7 41.♖g1 e4 42.♔g2 ♕f6 43.♖g3

White did not hurry at all and crushed Black by methodically continuing to improve his pieces. Black was just too tied down to put up much resistance.

Sometimes it is not clear which piece you should improve. What is a good square for your piece anyway? The answers to these questions can be very subjective. Depending on how your opponent continues, your 'improvements' may not even really be improvements.

But by trying to improve your pieces, you will definitely not spoil your position. And your play will have a level of consistency.

In the next game, Black beautifully improves his pieces with almost every move. Even though his pieces looked perfectly fine in the starting position, he finds better things for them to do.

D.Byrne-Fischer
New York 1956
position after 10...♗g4

White controls the centre and seems to be fine positionally, but Black is planning to play ...♘fd7 and ...e5 soon, after which he might simplify the position by undermining the white centre. So White tries to prevent ...♘fd7 as well.

11.♗g5? There doesn't seem to be anything obviously wrong with this move, and the temptation to prevent ...♘fd7 is understandable. But the bishop was perfectly fine on f4, and it was obvious that White still needs to finish his development. In such situations you don't look for problems and use a move like ♗g5 to avoid them. You just ask yourself: Can I improve another one of my pieces?

11.♗e2 would have been a perfectly normal move. Black could go ...♘fd7 and plan ...e5, probably equalizing without too many problems.

11...♘a4! This was certainly not easy to foresee, but if you follow simple guidelines like developing and improving your pieces whenever you can, it is much easier to spot such tactics.

12.♕a3 12.♘xa4 will be met by 12...♘xe4 13.♕c1 ♗xf3 14.gxf3 ♕a5+, and Black will win back the piece. It's incredible how easy it is to find tactical motifs against an undeveloped opponent...

12...♘xc3 13.bxc3 ♘xe4

We could stop here as far as our subject is concerned – but the next few moves contained a brilliancy that I can't resist sharing. Besides, the fluidity of Black's play again shows how useful development is in an open position.

14.♗xe7 ♕b6 15.♗c4 ♘xc3 16.♗c5 ♖fe8+ 17.♔f1 ♗e6!
An amazing tactic, although it wasn't the only way to get an advantage. Now White's position truly collapses.

18.♗xb6 Black has a clear advantage after 18.♗xc3 ♕xc5 19.dxc5 ♗xc3. And 18.♗xe6 ♕b5+ should lead to a smothered mate after 19.♔g1 ♘e2+ 20.♔f1 ♘g3+ 21.♔g1 ♕f1+ 22.♖xf1 ♘e2 mate.

18...♗xc4+ 19.♔g1 ♘e2+ 20.♔f1 ♘xd4+ 21.♔g1 ♘e2+ 22.♔f1 ♘c3+ 23.♔g1 axb6

And Black soon won all possible material.

Conclusion

If there isn't much in the way of tactics on the board, calculation is often useless. Instead, you should use your imagination and think about where your pieces would be well placed. A few questions that can help you choose the right squares for your pieces are:

1. Do I have any bad pieces?
2. Can I improve any of my pieces?
3. What plan would I like to follow, and can my pieces be better placed for that plan?

And lastly, before choosing a move, remember that it should not make any of your pieces worse than it was before. ∎

Solingen Returns

As the homogenous and ambitious team of Solingen ended the supremacy of star-studded juggernaut Baden-Baden in the German Bundesliga, **JAN TIMMAN** remembers a golden age.

For an entire decade, I was a member of clubs in Holland and Germany that were simply unbeatable and for many years dominated the leagues in both countries. It started in 1996, when textile merchant Henk Verstappen approached me in a bar in Wijk aan Zee and asked me to play for his Breda club De Variant. Shortly afterwards, Wilfried Hilgert, the big name behind Porz, invited me to come and boost his club's ranks. This was the start of our golden age. Regardless of whether I travelled to Breda or to Porz, we always had reasons to celebrate. The competition was fierce: in Holland from HSG Hilversum, the team sponsored by Joop van Oosterom; in Germany from Solingen, which could count on the financial support of the legendary Egon Evertz. The De Variant and Porz teams were homogenous groups with an excellent internal atmosphere, partly because Hilgert and Verstappen were such excellent hosts. After a match we always had a copious meal waiting for us somewhere.

In 2006, all of this suddenly stopped. De Variant lost its sponsors and eventually ceased to exist. In Porz, the situation was different: Hilgert decided to withdraw his first team from the highest league and entered his players at a lower level. This deci-

sion kicked up quite a dust, but Hilgert never provided a clear explanation. I think he just couldn't live with the idea of his club not winning the highest honour. Baden-Baden, meanwhile, had hired several very strong grandmasters. Could Hilgert not have done the same? In an interview with *Schach* at the time, he claimed that he had been offered Anand and Kramnik, but that he had declined the offer. Why?, the

> '**Paying some players considerably more than the rest disrupts the harmony in a team.**'

interviewer wanted to know. 'Because I found them too expensive', Hilgert replied. This was something I could understand. Paying some players considerably more than the rest disrupts the harmony in a team. In the meantime, however, we found ourselves playing under a cloak of anonymity.

This season we had a formidable competitor in DJK Aufwärts Aachen, which eventually finished second. This was enough for them to be promoted to the top league, since we continue to slog away in the lower regions. We are

fighting in the margins, but we continue to win, and when all's said and done, that's the only thing that counts.

In the top league, meanwhile, Baden-Baden had taken over the Marshal's baton with considerable fervour. Every year, sponsor Grenke Leasing puts together a team that would outclass any national team. Grandmasters from all over the world are flown in. As a result, the Bundesliga gradually lost all excitement and suspense. This year, however, another team carried off the spoils: none other than the old Solingen. Interestingly enough, Solingen had hit hard times when Evertz withdrew his sponsorship some years earlier, but two years ago, just when club president Herbert Scheidt was about to withdraw his first team from the league, an unexpected saviour announced himself. The *Solinger Tagesblatt*, in which I read about this, did not divulge the sponsor's name, but the club's website mentions five local companies, Stadt Sparbank Solingen amongst them.

This season, the team was led by Harikrishna, Rapport and Ragger, young and ambitious top players who made impressive scores. They were assisted by old hands Jussupow and Nikolic and the excellent Dutch grandmaster trio L'Ami, Van Kampen and Smeets. Rapport's games are always interesting. In the first round, he immediately left his calling card.

EO 42.4 – A34
Richard Rapport
Li Chao
Germany Bundesliga 2015/16 (1)
(SK Solingen-SK Schwäbisch Hall)

1.♘f3 ♘f6 2.c4 c5 3.♘c3 d5
4.cxd5 ♘xd5 5.e3 ♘xc3 6.bxc3
g6 7.♕a4+ ♗d7 8.h4

This advance has been known since
Keres-Polugaevsky, Riga 1968.
8...h5 Polu played 8...h6. Now the
white knight gets square g5. **9.♕c2**
A new move. White usually plays
9.♗a3, but Rapport wants to advance
his a-pawn before transferring his
bishop to a3. **9...♗g7 10.a4 0-0
11.♗c4 ♘b6 12.♗a2**

12...♗f5 The sharpest continuation.
13.e4 ♗g4 14.♘g5

14...a5
Both players have original ideas about
the game. With the text Black weakens his kingside in order to be able to
keep the knight on b6.
15.♖b1 c4 This advance boils down
to a pawn sacrifice.
16.♗a3 ♖c8 17.♖b5 White
declines. After 17.♗xe7 ♕xe7
18.♖xb6 ♖fd8 Black would have sufficient compensation for the pawn.
**17...♗d7 18.♖xa5 ♘xa4 19.♗b4
b5 20.0-0**

Having established a foothold for
his queen's rook in a curious way,
Rapport completes his development.
The position is equal, but White has
the easier play.
20...♕b6 A bad square for the
queen. Better was 20...♕c7. **21.d4
e5 22.♖b1!** To prepare a strong
exchange sacrifice.

22...♖fd8 Stronger was 22...♖fe8,
anticipating the exchange sacrifice:
after 23.♖xa4 bxa4 24.♗c5 ♕c7
25.♗xc4 Black would have been able
to defend with 25...♗e6.
The piece sacrifice 22...♘xc3 would
also have offered better chances than
the text. After 23.♕xc3 exd4 24.♕f3

♗g4 25.♕a3 d3 26.♖a6 White is
better, but things are not so clear-cut.
23.♖xa4! The point of the previous move. **23...bxa4 24.♗c5 ♕f6
25.♗xc4 ♗e8 26.♖b6 ♖xc5**
Black's only chance.

27.dxc5
White could have scored a brilliant win here, but it was hard to
calculate: 27.♗xf7+! ♔xf7 28.♖xf6
♗xf6 29.♘xf7 ♖xd4 30.♕a2! ♖xc3
31.♕e6!, and wins. This final move in
particular was hard to see.
27...♕e7 28.♕a2 Making the win
more difficult. After 28.♗d5! Black
would have been defenceless against
the threat of 29.♖b7.
28...♗f6! Now Black can still fight.
29.♗d5

29...♗xg5?
A blunder. After 29...♖c8 30.♖b7 ♖c7
31.♖xc7 ♕xc7 32.♗c4 White would
call the shots, but the black defences
would still be intact.
30.♖xg6+ Of course. Now White
will win easily.**30...♔f8 31.♖xg5
♕xc5 32.♖f5 ♕xc3 33.♗xf7
♕e1+ 34.♔h2 ♕xe4 35.♗g6+
♕xf5 36.♕a3+ ♔g7 37.♗xf5**
Black resigned.

Jan Timman

Harikrishna managed to score an extremely high 7½ out of 9 result against 2600+ opposition. There is a wide variety of wins to choose from, all of them worthwhile. In Round 6, he played a classical attacking game.

SI 20.5 – B81
Pentala Harikrishna
Robert Kempinski
Germany Bundesliga 2015/16 (6)
(SK Solingen-Hamburger SK)

1.e4 c5 2.♘f3 e6 3.d4 cxd4 4.♘xd4 ♘f6 5.♘c3 d6 6.g4 h6 7.h4

7...a6?
Kempinski had played this before, but in combination with his previous move this is a serious error. If Black was aiming for the central advance d6-d5, 7...♗e7 was the correct prepar-atory move. This has been common knowledge since the 1970s.

8.♖g1 d5 9.exd5 ♘xd5 10.♘xd5 ♕xd5

11.♗e3!
This is far stronger than 11.♗g2 ♕c4 12.c3 ♗e7, as in Azarov-Kempinski, Pardubice 2015. White wants to castle queenside as soon as possible.
11...♗e7 12.♕d2

12...♗xh4
This capture is normally very dangerous with the queens on the board, but the alternatives wouldn't have done either, e.g. 12...♘d7 13.♗g2 ♕c4 14.g5 hxg5 15.hxg5 ♘e5 16.0-0-0, and now 16...♕xa2 fails to 17.♘b3, with a decisive advantage.
13.♕c3 ♘d7 14.0-0-0

14...♕c5
More time-wasting. Black's only chance was 14...♗f6. Things look very bad after 15.♔b1, e.g. 15...0-0 16.♗c4 ♕c5 17.g5! hxg5 18.♘xe6! ♕e7 19.♕b3 fxe6 20.♗xe6+ ♖f7 21.♗d5!, with the devastating threat of 22.♗c5, against which there is no defence. Better is 15...♕d6, intending to withdraw the queen to e7, but Black's position does not exactly inspire confidence.

15.♕b3 ♕a5 16.♗g2 0-0 17.♖h1 ♘c5 18.♕c4 ♗e7

19.g5!
The thematic pawn sacrifice, which is already decisive.
19...hxg5 20.♖h2
White calmly doubles his rooks on the recently opened h-file.
After 20...♗d6 he has 21.♖h5.
20...f5 21.♖dh1 ♕a4 22.♕c3

22...♘e4
Desperation. After 22...♕xa2, 23.♖h7 would have been decisive.
**23.♗xe4 fxe4 24.♖h7 ♗f6
25.♖h8+ ♔f7 26.♖xf8+ ♔xf8
27.♖h8+ ♔f7 28.♕c7+ ♔g6
29.♕h2 ♔f7 30.♕c7+ ♔g6**

31.♖f8!

The most accurate rounding-off of the attack. White is threatening mate in two.
**31...♗d7 32.♖xa8 ♗xd4
33.♗xd4 ♕xd4 34.♖d8 ♕xf2
35.♕xd7 ♕f4+ 36.♔b1 ♗h7
37.b3 g4 38.♕e8 ♕e5 39.♖d1**

And Black resigned.

Both Baden-Baden and Solingen won their first eight matches and then squared up for a head-to-head. Baden-Baden had come at full fighting strength, out-rating its opponents on all eight boards by an average of almost 100 points. But they still didn't win: the result, after a pitched battle, was a 4-4 draw.

The homogeneity of the Solingen team was an important factor. Harikrishna wrested a draw as Black against Anand after a sharp Sicilian fight, while Rapport beat Aronian on Board 2.

Even more sensational things happened on Board 4.

Van Kampen-Wojtaszek
Germany Bundesliga 2015/16 (9)
(SK Solingen-OSG Baden-Baden)
position after 19.♕e5

White has a slight plus, although it doesn't amount to much. The computer now regards 19...♗b5 and 19...♖d8 as the most accurate moves.
19...♗c6
At best inaccurate, since it hands White a superior pawn structure.
20.♗xc6 ♖c8?
The point of the previous move. The white bishop is pinned, and Black is hoping to recapture on c6 with his rook. But White has a vicious riposte. Black should have settled for 20...bxc6, when White can claim a large advantage after 21.♕d6.

21.♖c4! Winning.
21...bxc6
This loses on the spot. Black had intended 21...♖xc6, of course, but Wojtaszek must have realized belatedly that this would allow White to

liquidate to a winning pawn ending with 22.♕b8+! ♔h7 23.♖xc6.

ANALYSIS DIAGRAM

The play could continue as follows: 23...bxc6 (otherwise White will take on a7) 24.♕xb6 axb6 25.a4 c5 26.♔g2! (not 26.♔f1 ♔g6 27.e4 f5!, and Black just manages to hold)

26...♔g6 27.♔f3 ♔f5 28.♔e3 ♔e5 29.♔d3 ♔d5 30.e4+ ♔c6 31.♔c4 e5 32.g4!, and Black is out-tempoed.

22.♖g4

Most unfortunately, 22...g6 now fails to 23.♖xg6+.

22...g5 23.♕f6

Even stronger than 23.h4, after which Black could still have tried 23...♕b5.

23...♕d8 24.♕xh6 f6 25.h4

Black resigned.

With wins by Svidler against Smeets and Bacrot against Nikolic, Baden-Baden managed to tie the match. A striking detail was that all victories in this crucial match were scored with the white pieces.

In the last six rounds, the fight between the two top teams remained tense. In Round 10, both Baden-Baden and Solingen won convincingly, but in Round 11, the Baden-Baden train got derailed: despite a considerable rating advantage on all boards, they were beaten 5-3 by Werder Bremen. This opened the way to overall victory for Solingen. They could even afford a little slip in Round 12, when they tied with USV TU Dresden. With three wins from the last three matches they convincingly clinched the championship. Solingen not only had one match point more than Baden-Baden, they also beat them by three board points.

It will be interesting to see what Baden-Baden will do next season to regain the title. Strengthening their team is virtually impossible, so Solingen can afford to be optimistic about next season, too. ∎

MAXIMize your Tactics Solutions

1. Safarli-Rasulov
Nakhchivan 2012

For checkmate along the back rank one major piece is needed. The rest is ballast. **36...♗d3+! 37.♖xd3 ♖g1+! 38.♔xg1 ♖b1+** White resigned.

2. Rathnakaran-Karthik
Bhubaneswar 2016

22.♕c3 ♕b4 Now Black's pieces are overloaded: **23.♘e7+!** and he resigned: 23...♖xe7 24.♕xg7 mate; 23...♘xe7 24.♕xb4; or 23...♔h7 24.♘xc6.

3. Gormally-Roberson
Birmingham 2016

23.♘xf5! The back rank motif: 23...♖xf7 24.♖d8+. **23...♕e1+ 24.♔h2! ♖xg2+ 25.♔xg2 ♗b7+ 26.♕xb7 ♖g8+ 27.♘g3** Black resigned.

4. Nikolova–Theissl-Pokorna
Germany Bundesliga 2015

41...♖xc3! 42.♕xf6 42.bxc3 ♗xc3 is checkmate. **42...♖c1+!** An essential interposition. **43.♖xc1 ♘b3+ 44.♔a2** 44.♔b1 ♗e4+!. **44...♘xc1+ 45.♔b1 gxf6 46.♔xc1 ♔g6** and Black won.

5. Karavade-Bailet
Nancy 2016

32...♖xb2+! 33.♖xb2 ♖xb2+ 34.♔xb2 ♕d2+ 35.♔b1 Or 35.♗c2 a3+! 36.♔b1 ♕c3, mating. **35...a3! 36.♕e2 ♕b4+ 37.♔a1** 37.♔c2 ♕b2+ 38.♔d1 ♕c1 mate. **37...♕c3+ 38.♔b1 ♗d2** and White resigned.

6. Ortega-Espinosa
Varadero 2016

25...♖xe3! 26.♖xe3 ♗d4 27.♘g2 Now 27...♗xg2 loses to 28.♖xd4, while after 27...♗xe3+ 28.♘xe3 White has an extra pawn in the ending. **27...♗c5! 28.♖de1 ♖f3** and Black won.

7. Willemze-L.van Foreest
Amsterdam 2016

26.♘f5 ♗h5 26...♘e8 27.♕h4+ ♔g8 28.♘h6+ and 26...♕xf5 27.♕xf5+ ♔g7 28.♖xe6 lose rather trivially. **27.♖xe6! ♗xg4 28.♖h6+ ♔g8 29.♗b3+ ♔f8 30.♖h8** Mate.

8. Bodnaruk-Chigaev
St. Petersburg 2016

32...♘f2+ 33.♔g1 ♘d3+ Not a smothered mate! **34.♕e3 ♖e8!** But 35.♕xd4 ♖xe1 is mate. **35.♗e6!?** Now after 35...♕xe3+ 36.♖xe3, neither of the knight moves is very convincing, so: **35...♖d8!** Now White sustains much heavier material losses.

9. Ipatov-Brkic
Gjakova 2016

27.f6? is premature due to 27...♕g4. **27.h4! ♕e8** 27...e4 28.♕f6+ ♔g8 29.♖f4; 27...♕d8 28.f6 ♖g8 29.♖xf7. Beautiful is 27...c3 28.h5 ♕d8 29.♖d7! (29.f6? ♕d2+) 29...♕xd7 30.♕f6+ ♔g8 31.h6 and White wins. **28.h5!** and Black resigned (28...♖g8 29.♕f6+ ♖g7 30.h6).

Nils Grandelius

CURRENT ELO: 2649

DATE OF BIRTH: June 3, 1993

PLACE OF BIRTH: Lund, Sweden

PLACE OF RESIDENCE: Malmö, Sweden

What is your favourite colour?
Red, for obvious reasons.

What kind of food makes you happy?
I eat everything, and am generally very happy.

And what drink?
Black coffee.

What was the best or most interesting book you have ever read?
Homage to Catalonia, by George Orwell.

What is your all-time favourite movie?
Rockers (1978) by Theodoros Bafaloukos.

What is your favourite TV series?
I very rarely watch TV-series, but probably *Father Ted* or something like that.

Do you have a favourite actor?
Hugh Fraser.

And a favourite actress?
Alicia Vikander.

What music do you like listening to?
Reggae music, of course.

What was your best result ever?
Winning the unofficial bughouse World Championship five years in a row, 2007-2011.

What was the best game you have ever played?
I quite enjoyed my game against Moiseenko in the Qatar Masters 2014.

Who is your favourite chess player?
Peter Leko, for the astounding clarity in most of his wins.

Is there a chess book that had a profound influence on you?
As a kid, I very much enjoyed *Grandmaster Preparation* by Polugaevsky.

What was the most exciting chess game you have ever seen?
All blitz games with commentary by Dmitry Komarov are unbelievably exciting.

What is the best chess country in the world?
It still has to be Russia, due to the very long tradition there.

What are chess players particularly good at (except for chess)?
Abstract visualization.

Do chess players have typical shortcomings?
We generally tend to take ourselves too seriously.

What is it that you appreciate most in a person?
Happiness.

What is it that you dislike in a person?
A sense of prestige.

Do you have any superstitions concerning chess?
I've found out that when you feel well, you tend to play well.

Who or what would you like to be if you weren't yourself?
Someone doing something beneficial for the planet.

Which three people would you like to invite for dinner?
Robert Nesta Marley, Josip Broz Tito and Indira Gandhi.

What is the best piece of advice you were ever given?
That results don't matter in chess – only the process of development is important.

Is there something you'd love to learn?
Discipline.

Where is your favourite place in the world?
I don't understand the question – chess can be played anywhere.

What is your greatest fear?
People without self-irony.

How do you relax?
By spending time with friends.

If you could change one thing in the chess world, what would it be?
Shorter time-controls. I personally don't like it, but I believe it's the only way forward for the sport.

What is the stupidest rule in chess?
The draw offer never really made any sense to me.

What will be the nationality of the 2050 chess world champion?
India, purely by numbers.

Is a knowledge of chess useful in everyday life?
Not the game itself, of course, but the qualities necessary to be a successful chess player are also useful qualities for everyday life.